AS A WOMAN

THINKETH

APOSTLE DR. YANA JOHNSON TORREGROSA MBE

www.dryanajohnson.com

ISBN: 978-0-9955105-0-0

First Printing: 2015

Photography By Richard Pascoe

For worldwide printing, printed in the USA

Apostle Dr. Yana Johnson Torregrosa MBE

www.dryanajohnson.com

info@dryanajohnson.com

TABLE OF CONTENTS

DEDICATION

This book is dedicated to God

with whom, everything is possible.

My father Keith Johnson for your unending love that left a bright light

in me to this day.

My earthly father who resembled my heavenly father.

My beautiful Angel Gabriela, to whom the Bible says we should leave an

inheritance.

My mum Cynthia Johnson, a woman of high standards.

The amazing man God sent to me,

Apostle Dr Eddie Torregrosa.

In loving memory of Beryl Dennis.

Acknowledgements

God gets the praise - Always!

I would like to express my gratitude to all the Apostolic Ministers who

have been a part of my prophetic growth, with special mention to;

Rose Wilmore,

Bishop John Mills

Apostle James Duncan

Apostle Dr Edrick Dublin

Apostle Frequency Revelator

and Tekka Nascimento.

These global icons relentlessly encouraged me on this prophetic journey.

Thank you for your love, guidance, and spiritual compasses.

FOREWORD

---

*A*postle Dr. Yana Johnson is a global Icon, prolific author and a renowned international speaker whom God has given an apostolic mandate to raise a new breed of five-fold ministers of the gospel. In this catalogue of divinely inspiring and provocative revelations titled, *"As A Woman Thinketh"*, Apostle Yana Johnson unpacks Throne Room revelations of how believers in the Body of Christ across the globe can be catapulted from the convictions of ordinary life of complacency and mediocrity to the realm of understanding who they are in Christ. In esoteric language, the author has successfully decoded the divinely coded mysteries on emotional healing which for ages have remained an inexplicable, implausible and unfathomable subject.

This book is a delicate recipe and the most relevant spiritual diet that will usher you into consistent streams of supernatural power invading the natural realm. This spectacular display of revelation knowledge in an area not so much talked about is what will culminate in a catalogue of jaw-dropping testimonies as humanity in the extreme quarters of life unreservedly partake of this fresh revelation which God is unfolding from the Throne Room.

Therefore, failing to get yourself a copy of this book is tantamount to setting up yourself for extreme disadvantage.

Are you emotionally wounded? Are you still lamenting over the degenerating dictums of the past disappointments and unmet expectations? Are you going through a rough patch in your life and lost at sea as to how to rise beyond the vicissitudes of life? This Holy Ghost-breathed book practically demonstrates how to decisively deal with negative situations and circumstances in life. It brims with provocative insights that provide a unique and ground-breaking entry into the process of spiritual growth and development. It is jam-packed with divine insights that will take you through a journey out of the convictions of ordinary life of complacency and mediocrity to plunge into the greater depths of spiritual understanding. The theologically challenging, deeply provoking and incredibly inspiring, hard-to-get revelations encapsulated in this book are set to revolutionize the course of your life forever. The depth and density of Throne Room revelations it contains requires the reader to make a conscientious effort to digest its morsels, hence it is not for those who are not ready to change.

This is such a provocative kind of book that will cause you to explode in the demonstration of God's power that will ruffle the feathers of those comfortable with the status quo and dazzle the minds of the masses.

Fore Word

Those who have pitched their tent in the valley of mediocrity and are sailing their boats through the shallow streams of spiritual understanding. It will launch you into an arena of the miraculous, to demonstrate God's power like never before. Metaphorically speaking, you are promenading on the brink of experiencing a whirl of extraordinary divine aura invading the natural realm, leaving the masses dazzled to the last degree. You are about to witness a factory of mind-blowing and jaw-dropping testimonies as the Body of Christ is catapulted to the dimension of the miraculous.

There is a new type of man to which this book is dedicated, who is emerging on the horizon and rising beyond the confines and limitations of the realm of senses to perambulate in an arena of divine exploits. Those who are comfortable with the status quo and have drowned themselves in the valley of religion will be dazzled in this critical hour as you are about to explode in the demonstration of God's power like never before.

With that being said, sit on the edge of your seat and fasten your seatbelt as the author takes you through an adventurous journey, to usher you into a catalogue of supernatural acts that will thrill you to the last degree!

Apostle Frequency Revelator (CEO: Global Destiny Publishing House & Global Resurrection Embassy Church)

PREFACE

And be not conformed to this world: but be ye transformed by the renewing of your mind, that ye may prove what is that good, and acceptable, and perfect, will of God.

(Romans 12:2)

*I*t is on the basis of this scripture that I am passionate to pour out the motivation from my heart. I have achieved a lot in my life as a recipient of a Queens Honor MBE (Member of The British Empire); winner of five business awards as an accomplished song writer; empowerment speaker; mother and surrogate to many whom I mentor. In retrospect to the above achievements, Romans 12 unveils the divine truth that we are not a product of our environment, but we create our environments from the Kingdom that lies at hand and 'within us', so to speak.

Colloquially speaking, I am very passionate about implementing values and principles that empower everyone I meet. As the word of God ascertains, we are called to be 'Salt and Light', in or out of season.

This means that at all times, we should have something of value from within us, to give, or to be a blessing to someone else. What we give is not a tangible substance per se but a spiritual blessing emanating from our matured personhood and character.

To provide a perspective on the historical background preceding the writing of this book, my journey began when my personal life was at it's lowest point. I was recovering from a traumatic emergency cesarean birth to my daughter, Gabriela.

I had just been told that I was to be made homeless and I had to move out within weeks of giving birth. This forced me to go back and live at my parents' home for three months. Returning home hurdled me back into my adolescent environment. I was back in my childhood room where memories of growing up created mixed emotions of frustration, detachment, rejection and even confusion.

Here I was, a new mum needing to be strong for my baby who needed me. I was so low to the extent that I didn't think I had enough survival reserves for the both of us as I was seemingly entrapped in a web of debilitating disorientation.

Preface

The grand finale of all my drama ended with a very traumatic event when my (then) husband abandoned me and became estranged in our marriage. He fell for the lure of worldly temptations and the false promises of them.

These three traumas happened all within the same year, a triple dose that exacerbated my plight and trust me into a morass of debilitating agony. It was the most traumatic time in my life ever, yet the most useful pain I have ever experienced. Overcoming such great pain was the fuel that accelerated me into my destiny.

In order for great things to be birthed and activated inside of you, God will allow great pain and even trauma, (that he can heal) to develop your character. He will teach you through this experience, to be compassionate, understanding and mature. Personal experiences will give you great authority in understanding how to overcome challenges and help someone else.

Such a combination of horrific events became a toxic formula that drove me to want to truly give up on my life. It was a borderline experience that set me on the edge of the cliff. A hairline string, just before insanity kicks in and claims you. This leads you to surrender everything you could ever do, or think, and completely let go to Gods true desire for you.

So, thats what I did. I simply let go. I stopped processing the what if's, and regrets. I stopped lamenting over the degenerating dictums of my life circumstances and set my gaze on possibilities. I stopped having expectations, desires and conditions. I just stopped. Finally, my mind was quiet.

Interestingly, during my time of stillness, I didn't break down, I just stopped. A break down is when overload causes manifestations of anger, screaming and outward signs of distress and overload. Yet something in me froze.

During that time, I was introduced to myself. My true state brought low, now exposed for me to see. For me to observe and I felt as though I was watching my own TV show where every reflection was magnified for inspection and a judgement. I felt totally lost. Embarrassed, rejected, unable to perform or do anything. I was broken on every level and most of all, abandoned. I cared no more because no one else did. I was detached and numb. Every trauma came to visit me.

All this drove me to find Jesus. Hallelujah!

A friend of mine Petra Johnson, had given me a devotional book called 'The Word for Today'. It had daily scripture and encouraging reflective text. At first, I wanted to decline, but I took it anyway and read it when I felt empty.

By the time I had completed reading my first quarterly issue, my perspective became clearer and I had stillness in my spirit from all of the trauma that I had experienced. The Bible says in Matthew 11:15 *let him who has an ear to hear, hear.*

I had run away. Left London and found myself back at the place I call home, where I am loved, trusted, understood and where I laugh. With my aunty Beryl. She is actually my cousin but I honor her because she didn't play favorites with me and my sister. She treated me fairly and called a spade a spade. If I was good I was praised and if not, scolded in love and that was it. No games, no in between or confusion. Just the truth. I always felt emotionally safe around her. She understood me and that was my peace. She is also a great encourager and a woman of truth.

I flew to New York, and went to stay with her. I always held a key for her apartment, wherever she lived. It was always my house too. I was there to heal. I was at peace, me and my, now toddler.

I would often fly to NY as a student on a work exchange program while at University. I found myself working on transfer from The Gap London to The Gap New York.

I eventually moved store to work at French Connection Broadway, where I had an entire street of friends from other retail stores who would meet after work to hang out in clubs or the latest place to be. New York was happy safe and fun. I loved being there.

After my work experiences which lasted for 2 years, I travelled back to New York as much as I could. I would look for the cheap deals on courier flights and turn up without notice. Often pushing my key in the lock of the apartment door, to the yells of excitement from my aunty who knew it was me surprising her.

Sometimes I would go to Washington Square Park with my friends and watch the Chess players. We would walk down 8th Street and look at shoes and explore the Village and the atmosphere of tourists and creatives. Me and my friends who were from Haiti had adopted me into their community, we had a great time.

It was a far cry from Birmingham and London and I felt recreated. When I was 9 years old, I found the Black Heritage section in my local library. I visited the library as much as I could, until I had read every copy of the Black History section.

There were authors like Toni Morrison, Maya Angelou, Toni Cade, Langston Hughes. I was mesmerized by the stories, autobiographies and collection of writers that I discovered, who were American.

Through these books, I was reliving the Harlem Renaissance and the Deep South. I was an artisan and had an inner voice that was given permission to speak. I was experiencing a connection to people and places that I could never know. Something inside of me was awoken.

I loved to write poetry. I loved to read. I now had inspiration. New York was it. The catalyst that changed me, just by being there. I developed as a New Yorcian. Since my experiences, I failed to fit into the British mindset. I had a different mentality. I didn't even realize it. But I was free to express myself. Not that anyone had said I couldn't, but there was an expression inside of me that insisted on coming out. This expression wasn't just my own opinion, it spoke for the community of those who were creatively free.

Prior to my visits to New York, I would write letters to let my friends know when I was coming in to town. On the day of my arrival, the phone would always ring off the hook. Aunty Beryl was always keen to answer the phone and when the boys would call, I would shout out, 'which one?' from the other room.

She would clear her throat and ask for further clarification, to prevent exposing my double dates.

Aunty celebrated our youth and gave me my sister and visiting friends, freedom and trust. We had fun, stayed safe and learned how to be responsible adults. We didn't always get it right but we learned. Aunty was very graceful.

When I reflect on the young people today, I believe that every young person needs an encounter that gives them a revelation of who they are. Whether its travel; missions; or serving as an apprentice. It can be a place where self discovery happens. Some young people struggle to develop their identity because they or their parents have not identified the truths about their lives. The baton has not been handed down and they are lost and disconnected from what is yet to be ignited within.

I have seen fear subdue a persons potential, robbing that person of the revelation of who they are and what they are capable of. It takes the maturing process; redefining our identity in Christ to know and walk in the truth of who we are. Ephesians 4:11 reads, *"And he gave some, Apostles; and some, Prophets; and some, Evangelists; and some, Pastors and Teachers, for the perfecting of the saints, for the work of the ministry, for the edifying of the body of Christ"*.

These are five leadership callings which empower the bearer of the gifts. They benefit those called to be leaders in the ministry of Jesus, through building the Kingdom Government in the Church body of believers.

My husband and I believe in commissioning those who we discern and see, function in these spiritual gifts. The commissioning blessing (Fathers blessing) activates what lies dormant within a person and brings them to life. Once they are activated, heavens identity partners with them and releases an anointing for them to achieve what they could not previously.

It had to be my third trip to the legendary, Brooklyn Tabernacle Church, in New York. It was the old BT building and the choir had just finished singing 'Use me Lord'. The previous two visits, quite by coincidence they had also sung the same song. I was overwhelmed with tears, again! This was a second time of surrender for me. But this time I really wanted God, with everything in me.

I held up my hand for prayer and in just a moment, I was saved from myself. Saved by Jesus from all of the ugliness that had surrounded me and infiltrated every sphere of human endeavor. In that moment, my life was redeemed by the price Jesus had already paid at the cross for me.

That was the day that the transaction was made and I was set free from every burden in my life, in an instant.

My day to day life however, didn't miraculously shift in to place instantaneously. It was just the beginning of a long journey with God. There was a shift in my life but because we live in a world dominated by God's timing, everything that was now perfect, took time to be restructured, healed and restored. I had to catch up with heaven and time and now walk in my blessing.

This is actually the principle of spiritual or physical healing. Some people are miraculously healed in an instant. However, many healings are fully complete in a moment and the fullness comes over time with continual faith.

This is how God healed my life, then and to this day. God heals our lives over the course of time. As we are transformed, others around us are also sculpted. We are all transitioned and are all continually developing and growing and maturing.

He is the potter and we are the clay! The process is faster than we think. As we heal and become transformed, others will provide confirmation through us to others, to provide evidence of His love for us.

My transformation happened in an instant but took many months to unfold. As my purpose began, I began to understand the limitations on my life as well as the liberties established for me to walk out what God has for me.

God wants us to connect with him so that he is the one joining us with whatever we need to for our lives. My full purpose of my life became evident as I began to depend on God. I developed a relationship in my heart and spirit. God wants to be acknowledged, he wants to be asked and he wants to be involved in every aspect of our lives. From the point when I understood this, every day was purposeful.

One thing is clear, none of this would have had happened if I had not renewed my mind every day. I grew by seeking and enquiring of God on practically everything, so that I could be transformed.

I didn't know or understand the Bible immediately. The quarterly devotional given to me by Petra was still my main inspiration and spiritual food. It was truth, and it was focused on Jesus and it transformed my heart.

My full potential wasn't obvious to me. I had to want to change, continually, every moment. It was a choice because I needed change, but most of all I needed God and more of him in every way I could find it.

Now He was very real to me and I had a vision of what I was destined to do. I began to want to walk in peace seeking after the reality of God but maintaining love, humility and forgiveness to others and myself. At that point in my life it was really hard. It was hard to forgive, I remember always asking, 'What did I do, that people would hurt me?'. I was the 'Why' person, always wanting an explanation.

I was confused at who would want to cause such pain to another person. I hadn't yet learned, that sometimes people are broken on the inside. If we are not mature enough to understand and choose the right people to love and honor us in relationships, then we will reap the harvest of their brokenness, immaturity and inability to nurture and love in return.

I struggled with this for a long time before I could heal and mature where my own heart could now have compassion for someone else without great expectation. It is my passion desire to raise up those who are *'Called'*, to help them understand their spiritual authority and to reach their full potential. I want people to realize that their potential is Leadership and that emotions will distract you, if you fail to mature.

This book will encourage and awaken the gift inside you.

Preface

'As a man thinketh, so is He', is the inspiration to write this book from my own journey (Proverbs 23:7)   Dr. Yana Johnson MBE

"Men do not attract that which they want, but that which they are. All that a man achieves and fails to achieve is the direct result of his own thoughts."

An excerpt taken from the book: As a man thinketh so is he by James Allen.

This is the essence of the law of attraction. As I sat and pondered in my quiet time, squabbling over the bones of my imagination, revelations crept into my spirit such that I felt compelled to bless someone else with.

I have gained much clarity. I have had much reflection over my life's circumstances. I know that this book will be a blessing and a time of intimacy. It is my deepest conviction that once you have inundated your spirit with a flood of revelations encapsulated in this book, you will get a clear understanding of your own life perspective and thus renew your mind accordingly.

This book is to renew, restore and release you into a new mindset.

CHAPTER ONE

SAVED TO SERVE

*I*t suffices to acknowledge that it really took a long time for me to embrace everything that has transpired in my life; a rhapsody of successes, challenges, changes and a very deep maturing process. Eventually, I recognized who and what God had called me to be. I can say this on behalf of many gifted individuals, who are effective on the outside appearance to others. The internal struggles in our private lives are very real and it can take a lifetime to understand ourselves.

Through all of my experiences, personal growth and development was inevitable. I refused to stand still or stay the same. There was a person on the inside being developed, which was not something you would see from the outside. Every now and then, tiny glimmers of hope, achievement and capabilities would be visible.

Still, I had yet to believe that I was capable of great things and own it despite the rags and threads of my torn life.

I needed to know deep down inside that I am destined for greatness. I embraced, every new challenge that arose. It took a very long time to realize that this is all part of Gods training. Not only did God do something special in my life in divinely translating me into his eternal Kingdom, He really did put something special in me as a person, His DNA.

As corroborated by the scripture, some of these gifts were divinely embedded in the inner recesses of our being right from my childhood. It's just that they had not yet been unwrapped. Figuratively speaking, guess what God did? We had Christmas and he unwrapped every gift in front of me spiritually and I could see them one by one, as it were. There was something special on the inside.

I had to then test them and learn the manifestation of every gift. I had to go through the challenges of life. This phase is very difficult because in the test, your gifts are ridiculed, laughed at, accused and even rejected. This happens so that you are sharpened and developed under strong conditions so that you can withstand anything that attacks you. When you experience true transformation, you don't forget it and every part of the testing process stays with you as a tool for your mature leadership role that you are being developed for.

This appears to be a cruel way to give a gift. Every gift is eternal and for the benefit of our destiny and Kingdom building. We are to build up others and become great stewards of not only our own lives but to the next generation. Our gifts, have to be tried and tested. That way, when they are handed down they continue to be eternal. They get handed down with potency to every generation that can never be watered down.

This is true of Gods power, Gods love and Gods spirit. Every generation gets a portion and it never weakens. Spiritual gifts work alongside the Kingdom principals God has established for us. When we successfully walk in the fullness of our DNA in Christ, we see our true inheritance through our gifts. The world accepts our gifts as they benefit the Church. God is glorified as he is the one who has given them to us. We are created to Worship God. When we achieve and live in the fullness of our gifts, our lives become a worship to God.

It may have been in one single moment. It may have been over a period of time, However, I noticed that the ability to encourage and empower people was given to me. As I have shared my story all over the world, I realized that many people have gifts inside them which remain dormant.

When I mentor others, we awaken their gifts by recognizing them and activating them. Calling them out with spiritual authority and commissioning those who we have identified as five-fold ministers.

God has empowered my husband and I, to raise up the five-fold ministry & gifts as in Ephesians 4:11. My husband and I have witnessed people growing from strength to strength. When a person knows their identity in Christ, they have the confidence to start their ministry and walk in their calling. When a person has been commissioned, it connects them to their ministry calling. Their DNA is activated and they experience a spiritual thrust to start their ministry.

Recognizing this activation in people's lives, encouraged me. It confirmed to me, that there is a calling on my life. After ministering to people. The transformation that I witnessed in their lives became a frequent outcome. Looking back on how God saved me to serve Him, I often felt inadequate and ill equipped. God had chosen me to be a blessing to others. From the tatters of what I had experienced in my life, God had used those experiences to strengthen me and empower me to have authority in those same areas.

God has chosen many of you reading this book also. There is something stirring on the inside of you that is lying dormant that needs activating.

There is a sleeping giant on the inside of you that need to be awakened. Often people would confirm the outcome of something I had prayed or prophesied over their life. They would testify of what God had done for them, after receiving prayer. These confirmations were random at first, but then became more consistent. When you least think that you are qualified, you are in fact endorsed and qualified.

God delights in us, when we step outside of ourselves and look beyond our own emotions. He wants us to let go of the limitations that hold us back in our minds and reach out to someone else. Despite how inadequate you may feel, it is there, the greatest miracles happen.

It is important to note that miracles do not happen where they are needed but rather where they are expected. Miracles happen when there is a great expectation. Expectation gives birth to the miraculous. That is why when you stretch out your hand in faith, it is actually God's hand that completes the work he has called us to because he gives grace for us to finish and start the task.

His work is done through us. God saves us so that we can serve Him.

NEED TO FORGIVE

My family upbringing was normal, so to speak. Just like any other family, it had its fair shares of ups and downs, acceptance and rejection. The strain was sometimes too much to handle. I experienced many challenges, to the extent that sometimes isolating myself was a way of coping. At that time, I considered such a motion as the best solution under the circumstances. Without the knowledge of God, his DNA in me and understanding what I am called to, I would run away from the very things I needed the most.

We do not all develop in an environment of unconditional love and forgiveness. Instead, we function out of a place of our emotions, especially when you carry a prophetic gift. You are very sensitive and until maturity settles your character, life is very turbulent.

My gift was unidentified and I came to learn that many prophetically gifted people suffer rejection. However, when they have matured, their experiences are used to bring people out of the darkness, caused by their actions and reactions. Often people reap the fruit of seeds they have sown in decisions they have made based on their sensitive and defensive behavior.

When you have a relationship with God, there is no intimidation and manipulation in your life. Truth becomes a very present driving force to your critical thinking and you see people through the eyes of Jesus, with unconditional love. You see people's potential and you see whats blocking them. Your unconditional love will want to heal them with the same heart as Jesus.

Truth creates a new perspective that is not flawed by fear or anything that would manipulate what you see. Maturity begins with truth, both inward and outward. The way you see yourself and accept truthfully who you are, is how you begin to understand others instead of by your own expectations.

With truth, you can be yourself, you are free, 'saved', from opinion and preference. You are finally able to live in the fullness of who you are, and who you become as God transforms you daily. Your old personality gets renewed on a daily basis and you become better and better each day as old habits and weaknesses fall off.

You become healed and your life is no longer controlled by falsehood. This should be your desire, that you grow in the belief of who Christ is in your life and who you are in His.

I didn't know about the five- fold ministry, I didn't know I carried a prophetic gift, so I just listened to the voice of the Holy Spirit and did what he said to do.

It is years later that I realized where my independence and confidence came from. The Holy Spirit was always there, teaching me what to do. He was always speaking to my spirit and bringing insight and wisdom. If you listen to what the Holy Spirit says to do and you are obedient, He will prosper you greatly.

Your new personality in God attracts people. The good things God has in store for you will allow you to be proactive instead of reactive. When unconditional love is missing from our lives, we are easily offended and we hold grudges against those who have offended us. We allow the offense to shut down our ability to interact, and forgive beyond that single offense.

Have you ever noticed how a sincere apology wipes away hurt and you can move forward? Well, try to put an apology in place for someone who has hurt you and see how quickly their offensive nature is now an understood.

Understanding that doesn't change them, but it changes the impact they have on you. This is unconditional love.

Accepting what you cannot change everything but by embracing God, He will change everything, is a great place to start. I had to learn this. Without it I would perish with a bitter heart.

The open state of our heart allows transformation to be possible. We are constantly tested by people in and around our lives. When people are no longer perceived because of negative things in our life, then we are in a great place of maturity, healing and grace. No person has the power to do anything you don't allow.

We should be able to forgive, dust off the shackles of the past and focus ahead. Embracing principles of truth and compassion and love establish great authority. When we try to achieve results in our emotional and spiritual life without the knowledge of the spiritual tools available to us, we fail. We need help to accomplish the purpose for which God has designed for us to achieve.

We become frustrated and blame something or someone. The tools or principles of God are maturity and coping mechanisms which respond to people and situations through Gods eyes. I have found that they never fail when we apply the tools in the relevant situations.

Our maturity on the earth comes from our readiness to fully submit to Gods voice and do things the way he would. He is always talking to us and will guide us, if we pray and ask him. He wants to heal us and change our thinking from selfish to His Kingdom thinking. He wants to reform our minds into his mind. When we are really in him, so much other stuff will no longer matter.

The lies of the enemy will tell us that we should cut someone off who doesn't agree with us, but Gods heart says pray for them, give it to me. Let me transform them. Matthew 5:44 says *Love your enemies and pray for those who persecute you.*

At the root of our own truth we find our self. We realize that someone must have had to endure our flaws. We begin to recognize how we are designed to overcome the challenges that come our way, ultimately designed to make us grow. We have to do it in spirit and in truth. Even though change happens over the course of our lives, we can, in fact, go back over time and heal that limitation from off our lives.

We can reflect on our memory and accept what is ours to accept. We can place purpose for everything that has happened to us, owning up to what belongs to us and be responsible by taking control of what happens next.

We are not victims of life circumstances. The negative situations that occur in our life, is not someone else's fault, no matter how much the impact is. We should not feel guilt or condemnation when something bad happens in our life at the hands of someone else. Although the cause of our pain is an uncontrollable one, what we choose to do with our emotions is 100% our own. Forgive, then move on. Repent then move on. Every stage of the circumstances that we go through in life is designed to help us grow and develop, it is our learning curve.

A successful life is the result of what we choose to do with our circumstance, which also reflects our level of maturity. How we respond to life's challenges is a reflection of what we have learned about ourselves. We can see the glass as being either half full or half empty. When we know the truth about ourselves, it will set us free from condemnation, from other people's opinion and from taking on a false identity that does not represent us as the child of Christ.

We can be affected so deeply that psychologically causes trauma to remain in our emotions for a very long time. This trauma can be triggered by actions that cause negative memory to replay in our minds. Until we have learned to be still and confident in who we are, we can find ourselves repeating negative responses which ultimately limit our lives.

11

As we interact with others, they may do something that triggers a part of our memory which results in us giving a negative response to them. We may well retaliate due to emotional limitations that create short tempers, impatience and division and disagreement which leads to isolation and ineffective unforgiving life. As the scripture ascertains, the enemy comes to steal Kill and destroy all that we are designed to achieve in unity. His plan is to divide and conquer.

Our emotions can become protective of our spirit. Trying to prevent trauma and avoiding interaction to protect ever being traumatized again, instead of developing the skills to confront and overcome. When we remain immature it causes us to forfeit growth and it ends in division. When we run away from the process designed to sharpen us, we start back at square one. If you find yourself going round the mountain again and again, ask yourself, *'What lesson have I not yet learned?'*.

Subconsciously, the age we experience trauma, is the age we remain emotionally broken until we are truly healed and that trauma is resolved. Our subconscious memory causes us to continually protect our spirit and live a somewhat limited life until we experience true and full healing. When we have matured, our responses will be the reflection of the fruit of the spirit and govern how we react.

Every physical age has spiritual development attached to it. When each age has not been fully resolved (graduated) there is an emotional blockage attached to the spirit at that age point. For example, when someone grants you an apology. No matter how long ago the offense. Once the apology has been granted. The memory of the pain dissolves, to the extent where reconciliation can occur.

If for example you were hurt at aged 13, you will react in a 13 year olds mental capacity in some instances, until that trauma has been resolved. Unresolved issues of a 13 year old adolescent will manifest when triggered.

When praying for people, The Holy Spirit has sometimes revealed to me the emotional age that a person suffered trauma. On investigating what happened, their full story is revealed and prayer can be ministered, healing that trauma.

I can administer healing to traumatized people and pray over spiritual blockages on a persons life that can be broken with specific prayers. Complete emotional trauma and healing takes place when the fear attached to the trauma is exposed and legal right reinstated. Fear cannot hide when the anointing of God is present.

The anointing, is Gods dispensed Dunamis power sent through Jesus, then to man and is capable to break the spiritual strongholds of bondage through the person sent to pray for you. After that prayer healing comes and the person is completely set free of the hindering spiritual blockages that prevents a full life in Christ.

Once truth is unlocked, that which was once creating oppression now stands on the new truth, opression will not function on the truth of God. When you are set free from limitations and oppression, you do not have to have to yield to limitations again. The spirit man becomes empowered and trauma has to leave. The Bible says in James 4:7 *Resist the enemy and he will flee.*

The root of our own truth is usually a very good place to start. I have seen people spend countless amounts of money on self-help programs and personal development. The truth will set you free; free from condemnation of self and from others.

When we manage our memories and the history of our lives in a truthful way, embracing our fears and failures and owning up to what is ours to own up to, we Kickstart a healing process to becoming whole. It will cause us to see our own faults as well as those who we could easily blame.

No matter what God puts us through, he is activating something inside of us to reach higher and dig deeper and form a character that has been tried and tested and resembles his nature.

When we are healed and can talk about our situations without the hurts and anger and negative emotions flaring up, we begin to grow as we realise who we truly are. Our testimonies become a platform of empowerment for those who hear it. It can be used as a tool to help someone else get through a challenge, knowing that God has a strategy to mature us spiritually and allow us to face challenges and overcome them as they arise.

Forgiveness is our choice. Forgiveness to another who has hurt us is for our own spiritual health. It teaches us to let go. Releasing the perpetrator from our negative thoughts and allowing Gods peace to present itself where we are weak.

If we cannot forgive, we ultimately suffer the hardship of reminding ourselves of our own unchanging and bitterness. We regurgitate every detail of why we should remain bitter and unforgiving to the person who hurt us and we hold ourselves in bondage of our own negative emotion and the offense we experienced.

Sometimes people hurt us unintentionally. Not being able to forgive a person prevents us from moving forward in real love and truth we are designed to. Forgiveness is not for the benefit of the other person. Forgiveness allows our own mind and heart to let go of hurt and keep our hearts clear of emotional junk. We need to be able to allow good and bad to pass through our lives. This will enable our growth and ability to continually move forward. It will give us the ability to take dominion over that which we don't like and that which we do.

Unforgiveness, occurs when we feel that we are not able to manage disagreements or communicate effectively so we shut down and remain closed to the issue. When we mature, we can talk things through, share the Kingdom principles that bring liberty and remain unaffected by emotional hurts. Our bodies, hearts and minds belong to God therefore everything we experience is His experience too.

Protecting every experience simply keeps us closed to being vulnerable and shuts God out, instead of placing Him in the place of our High Priest, King and Provider. If we fix everything then we leave no room for him to fix anything at all. If we cannot be vulnerable, we forfeit a true relationship. God is our Plan A and he doesn't want us to function from our Plan B.

Forgiveness is not giving any blame to the perpetrator rather releasing our own mind and bodies from entertaining guilt, anger and hurt which, if not dealt with will cause disease in our own minds, bodies and emotions.

If we cannot forgive, we become bitter and judgmental and closed. We begin to speak negatively, think negatively and push people away who do not agree with us. This is the beginning of isolation.

The enemy comes to steal, Kill and destroy and in dividing us we end up in isolation. We then slowly die spiritually from the true impact we are to have coexisting within a community of those who know God and impacting those who don't. God designed it that way so that we each would have something interesting to share with each other. Matthew 13:24 speaks of the parable of the wheat and the tares. If we do not know who we are in Christ then in our immaturity we cannot function with the first family we are adopted into in our local church. If we cannot function there, then we will not have impact to effectively engage and attract anyone else, who doesn't know Jesus. They will look at our behavior and our mindset and reject Christ based on what we demonstrate as people who know Gods Love.

If you have experienced a negative behavior from someone who claims to know Jesus, just know that they are still going through a process of development in their own lives. Although they are sent to be a true witness of who he is. If you get to know Jesus for yourself, you will see and understand the person better.

When you are isolated, your world becomes Black and White, it becomes very insular and you literally cut yourself off from the fullness of life you deserve to have. The only person who hurts is yourself. It is your responsibility to persue the healing of your heart.

Sometimes we act out of fear or protection, that someone might hurt us, so we create walls that no one can permeate our hearts. We remain broken, unable to bond in relationships and enjoy a full life. A behavior pattern of brokenness that continually rejects love, results in isolation. It places you outside of a community that has the ability to Love and nurture you.

We cannot paint everyone with the same brush, therefore we must remain open to learn and love who ever God has designed to come into our lives for a season or a lifetime. In return, we will receive the same graces. We will reap that which we have sown and more.

To find your healing, you have to be deeply honest with yourself and acknowledge where you have played a part. You may have accepted something negative into your heart without realizing. If you haven't, then the hurt you are experiencing means you must forgive yourself first. Dig deep and allow God to reveal the root of your thoughts and problems as a result of your negative experience.

Despite your experiences, you are no less the person who God has called you to be and in fact, your development and healing will be powerful in helping someone else in the very place you have struggled.

Sometimes we allow the perceptions of others to hold us back. Sometimes it is something someone has said. As we go through our emotional development there will be a time of breakthrough when memories no longer hold our emotions captive. We will begin to identify with others who may have experienced similar circumstances. Our strength can be an encouragement to them. Our experience can be a helpful compass for moral guidance. The fact that we have survived is an encouragement to someone else, proving that you can make it through the most difficult times in your life.

As we mature and continue to heal from our past hurts, we reach a level of maturity to encourage and nurture others who have just begun their journey. Understanding another person takes courage, it takes humility and it takes an open heart, because although you feel as though you could help them, they might not be open to you initially. However, as you mature, you will be able to see past their limitations and extend love and friendship regardless of what you might get back. You too were once broken and closed in your hurt. When you are healed of offense, you are not easily offended. Offense is designed to divide.

Humility allows us to have understanding and it allows people to see their own behavior through patience and non judgement. It allows them to consider moving past their fear and pain and equips them to address the issues which keep them closed in their own minds. Healing from an offense takes time. Humility is always a great attitude to have when healing from offense. Knowing that God is our defender, healer, advocate, and comforter.

Tell yourself, 'It's not up to me!', and watch how God redeems that hurt and makes you strong in that area. One day you will look back and realize how far you have come. One day you can be grateful for experiencing your hurt because you will realize how it has made you stronger.

God does not always operate on our expected timing. When through humility there is healing, it brings you closer to God, knowing more about your own heart and how God has designed it.

Allowing God to work through our hearts is important because we realize how powerful we are through him. The ability to heal, forgive and let go, is a choice but with the help of God it is a purposeful choice with no regrets. God uses the pain in that experience to empower us and nothing is lost. The exchange of humility, embarrassment, fear and pain is replaced with Love, Power and a sound mind. These gifts now sharpened and activated, Ready to be used over and over again to defeat every glimpse of fear and overcome every challenge, mentally, emotionally and physically. Empowered through the mind of Christ.

Humility breeds love. Choosing humility is higher thinking, where you focus on a positive outcome and result in a positive outcome. As you do this once you will be amazed at how easy it is to stay peaceful within yourself. This attitude allows you to develop an open heart to understand the root cause of someone else's behavior or mindset, yet still love them and overlook their shortcomings.

We need to understand others and not become offended by them. We must remind ourselves that they are where they are because of a weakness in them that can be healed with time. We must not to take things personally and harbor offense but at all times recognize that the offense others can sometimes hold, is not because of something you have said or done. Remaining grounded and connected to Jesus, prevents people projecting their hurt on you. You have the power to allow or disallow hurt into your heart. When you are burdened, pray and tell Jesus, He will heal you to love unconditionally.

There is a saying that, 'Hurt people, hurt people!' This is because when we are hurt we can react out of any of the 5 stages of grief; denial, anger, bargaining, depression and acceptance. This is the emotional process to begin dealing with loss or disappointment. Often in this emotional process there is anger and frustration, just looking for a place to rest. These emotions govern the way we think and the way we think governs the way we act. The way we act is our identity, 'who we are for as long as we are doing it'. The bad news is that, it can produce negative results, the great news is that, we can change it, immediately! We can take control because we have authority over our own minds.

What triggered my heart to write this book is firstly overcoming many challenges in my life until I achieved a higher level of peace; love and understanding and forgiveness.

Secondly, I recognized how hurt and offended people were all around me and thirdly that maybe, my gift of empowerment could change someones life, simply by pouring out what I have learned and experienced. By sharing how Gods Holy Spirit has whispered his wisdom and into my heart, changing me forever. Lack of forgiveness almost robbed me of an incredibly abundant and fruitful full life. Until it was dealt with.

I often questioned God, How and Why was I nominated for such pain and hurt. I was quickly reminded of Luke 12:48 *To whom much is given, from Her much is required.* It is indeed a privilege to see this principal come to fulfillment in my life. Its promise honors me as I continue to trust in God. Many times, I am challenged again and again in different ways, but the approach to overcoming must remain the same.

John 15:4 Says, *As I abide in Him, He abides in me".* Love, Joy, Peace Kindness, Meekness, Self control, Humility, Long suffering are all the characteristics of Gods spirit in us.

Until we apply humility, no solution comes. I have seen disagreements turn into arguments that cycle round and round and came to no resolve simply because humility is absent and pride has taken its place. We live in a society whereby, most want to be heard, recognized. Sometimes we are not forthcoming when the shoe is on the other foot and we are selected to be the listeners instead of the speakers. All take and no give. This is a big set up for failure and negative conflict.

The way you think, will ground you and form a strong foundation that nurtures peaceful outcomes. We can choose to shift the dynamics of our lives from negative outcomes to positive outcomes. We can make room for the opinion of others and we can choose to serve, empower and enlighten from what we understand of the perspective of Christ.

Sometimes, even those who have a pure heart can find themselves offended because of the actions of another. Responses that are motivated by love and a servant heart allow and encourage patience and understanding to surface when issues arise.

We are reminded in the Bible to renew our minds daily, therefore as each situation happens.

This simply means that we can willingly submit to take a fresh approach and not allow negative behavior to hinder our future thoughts or actions. We can become the change we want to see, by being servant leaders.

We control our own minds and thoughts at all times. We have authority over our memories and can at any time submit them to God for healing and to help us to walk empowered.

I decree and declare that by virtue of reading this book, you will find healing when you submit your hurts to the Lord Jesus Christ. He died that you might live. He delights to see you get up, dust yourself off from whatever card life has dealt you and walk upright in Him. It is never too late and there is NO condemnation as shared in Romans 8:1. The past is past and all things are made new.

Your testimony will be great and you will be able to talk about your situation that will heal, empower and release someone else from mental bondage. This book will bring understanding, clarity and encouragement to remind you that it is your right to search for healing and peace and it is God's grace love and desire that you find it.

The Bible says in Revelation 12:11 that, "*We overcome by the blood of the lamb and the word of our testimony.*" Which in essence is PROOF that there is power in the name of Jesus. The very reason that Jesus died for our sins was so that we could have power and authority. He has given us the ability to shift our mindset that we might become healed and whole. He wants us to inherit the power through His Holy Spirit into our spirit to make us strong and do the marvelous works that Jesus had done when he was on the earth and more.

We cannot give what we haven't got therefore, Jesus's desire is for us to become whole, so that we can impact others to becoming whole. He came as a template to show us by example. All we have to do is follow his example.

God desires that every generation do more than the last, even more so because in every generation there is light and darkness. As the darkness tries to increase, with every generation, God raises up people to be His light that they will change their environments, in the knowledge of Him and in the full truth of how he has designed us to defeat everything negative in this world.

God is all Glorious.

God wants to pour this miraculous power into your life and activate spiritual gifts in your spirit which will allow you to achieve so many things on the earth. God told us in Genesis 1:28 to subdue the earth, which means to take by authority, to 'take forcefully'. This represents being dominant, strong, and powerful. With the authority to see a need and be able to make a change practically and spiritually with the compassion of Jesus.

We were made to glorify God on the earth, knowing who we were called to be. We are called to undo the works of darkness by walking in our authority and using the power bestowed to us to activate change in our environments. Change where people have been held captive through deception, where they are estranged from the heart of Jesus and do not know who they are or what they are called to do. It is the responsibility of those who do know who they are to help find them and build them up to grow into mature world changers.

If we could just move ourselves and emotions out of the way, get over ourselves and our mental blockages and limitations, then there we would see God move in our lives. It would be evident to others in a tangible way and inspire them of who God is, in a practical way.

Many people have low self esteem, low mood, low mindset, that literally manifests dysfunction during times in their life. Diseases and depressions that paralyze people in the prime of their life leaving them unable to do anything of impact for themselves or for anyone else. They have been robbed of their identity in Christ. They have been robbed of His love.

Some of these limiting traumas happened during their youth, some because of their innocence and the inability to defend themselves. Trauma can may even have been caused as a result of someone else's fear, jealousy or inability to love, nurture and protect you when they should have done. The enemy of our souls knows that if we are disconnected from the source of Jesus Christ, then we will look elsewhere for love, acceptance, approval and validation. We will look in all of the wrong places and end up with the wrong results.

When we search for our identity with a broken mindset, we really are incapable of forming truthful trusting transparent relationships. When failure comes and disappointment presents itself, we can are hard on ourselves, and label ourselves unlovable, to the point where we become self destructive.

The enemy uses our thoughts to destroy us, which ultimately destroys others by creating many layers of hurt all over again. We then easily duplicate negative instead of positive.

In a broken state we may even allow others to disrespect us and treat us less than we deserve to be treated because we are not strong enough to defend our hearts. We accept less than we should in search of validation, in search of belonging.

We need to reconnect to our heavenly Father, who designed us and who can repair us in a better state than when we first approached him.

God is love. He came as Love and conquered death by rising from the grave after 3 days. Through love, he cannot be held captive. God owns captivity! He is captive in our hearts and only through the hearts of those who desire His pure love, will His pure love flow.

The Bible says in John 14:6, that *no one can come to the Father except through Jesus.* It is the acceptance of Jesus, that love is released in abundance so that when we approach God, we are recognized by him.

We are simply required to believe on Him, and in Him to usher in salvation, so that we can be 'saved' from our ignorant state and receive His life-giving grace.

The salvation of Jesus Christ can come directly through Him by faith or through someone else encouraging you, speaking or singing of Him.

Faith comes by 'Hearing'. Is He calling you? Do you hear Him? It's not a trick question, or a psychological trick. Gods voice is a still small voice, either you hear it or feel it in your spirit, or you don't.

If you do, then respond! Simply tell Him you believe in Him and ask Him to transform your life and your ways. Acknowledge that because you were not in Him and that He was not in You, you were, in fact, a sinner. Ask Him to explain and to talk back to you through your spirit and He will. Apologize and tell Him that you do believe.

It's that simple. If by any chance you do this exercise and feel like you are not connected, then do it again and again until you hear Him in your spirit. His voice can sometimes sound like your own voice and that's okay.

The Bible says in Jeremiah 31:33 that *the new covenant was written on the heart of man*. That means although it can be helpful for someone to lead you to Him, He is capable of connecting with you totally himself. He is real.

Your heart is designed to hear him. It has been designed by God that you share His DNA, even if you don't believe in Him now, He is still your creator. He wants you to choose Him. He has given you free will. That way you will know its a pure connection. No strings, Just pure, sincere Love!

I encourage you to have a truthful, sincere conversation in faith with God, whom you cannot see or touch. When He actually acknowledges you, then you will see and then you will hear and you will know for certain that there is a God.

When we have the Holy Spirit inside of our minds, hearts and soul we feel his communication, His still small voice whispering into our soul, then you can receive the spiritual gifts he has for you and use every gift he has given to you.

You will be stirred to pray. You will be stirred to talk to Him and pour out your heart. You will have an awakening that he is real and that you actually belong to him.

God will guide you into all truth and the spiritual gifts will help you. This is the blueprint that started the early Church, this is how the Church body grew.

'We ARE the Church'. We are designed to hear his voice, nothing of that blueprint template has ever changed to this day!

For every generation that has lived in the knowledge of God, every generation has received the same potency of His love and power. The real DNA and heartbeat of Jesus, does not require pumping up or dressing up, it is pure truth for ever and ever.

In the Bible, we read that signs and wonders happened by the hands of those who believed in Jesus. It is still the same today, but we need restoring back to that truth and intimate communication that reconnects us with how we were created. We will be reconnected to listen in the spirit and then respond, from whatever the voice of God says to do.

When we acknowledge Jesus Christ in truth it triggers a sincere repentance of sins, which draws us closer to Him and the scales of pride and issues of life fall away. We are drawn into his marvelous light, an illuminated understanding of Him in us.

When we have made that connection of truth, then there is a downpour of spiritual gifts into our spirit which completes something in us.

We are then gifted to teach, pray for others and communicate life with an understanding of authority in Christ and the mandate he has given us here on earth. We connect with our destiny.

We call this equipping and it allows us to win others to the Lord and make provision on this earth to others through the ability to understand and mentor them from our own journey. As a Christian we have a job to DO, we have been equipped.

We have been given the tools and we are taught how to use them for full effect (success). When you are fully equipped and have the Holy Spirit dwelling in your heart, then everything you do yields amazing results.

It makes it easy to speak about Jesus, to unbelievers and it also gives you the ability to withstand rejection and hardship, because you realize that you are not being rejected but the Christ in you is.

For some people, personal reflection and looking inward is painful and hard. Sometimes people do not want to hear about God because they have a false sense of security hiding behind the lies that dominate their lives.

They do not want to be challenged to change. Therefore, they reject the message of Christ and the messenger along with it.

Sometimes it is very hard for others to understand especially if they are still brokenhearted and cannot allow their emotions to be healed. The promise of anything good can be rejected. We are empowered and encouraged to pray for them.

As I mentioned that when I had the understanding of Ephesians 4:11, I was then connected to the truth of who I was and my identity in Christ. I was able to see my own flaws and the grace on my life given to me by God to achieve many things despite my flaws.

So, I began to correct them. Compassion welled up inside of me to have more patience, kindness, understanding and forgiveness and unconditional love for others.

Painful memories grew dim as I was being changed. The broken relationships of the past are now completely healed. Only God can sort out the mess we get ourselves into so that we can focus on His message through our experiences. Lots of praying, humility and forgiveness is a great place to start with the mess in your life.

A CALL TO LEADERSHIP

$\mathcal{Y}$ou can be the entrepreneur of your own life and then using that template, literally, start anything you desire. When Gods DNA is in you, you begin to want what He wants for your life and he longs to give us the desires of our hearts. The five-fold ministry is not about a title, but more about what the title is designed to do.

The Kingdom of God is a spiritual mindset of a higher thinking, requiring us to love and nurture those in our lives and community. There is a physical Kingdom of God also. Our first pillar of understanding is that faith (things we cannot see) forming an attitude that God's principles can be exercised in faith and then the reality is formed. When we know the measure of gifts people carry, especially when they have been healed from mindsets of old trauma, we can nurture them to grow and flow in their gift.

According to Kingdom principles, we help them to live prosperous lives which positively impact others through knowing who they are and how their authority functions. Their transformative redemptive authority becomes evident, based on the area in their lives that they have overcome.

When you have overcome something in Christ, your authority in that area is very great and will be dynamic to set others free, based on that 'Testimony'. The Bible says in Revelation 12:11 that *we overcome by the Blood of the lamb and the word of YOUR testimony*. Proof to the courts of heaven that Jesus's authority works to this very day. The same resurrection power that rose Jesus from the grave is still at work through you and with the same authority and power that he gave you through the blood shed at the cross at Calvary. Praise His name.

If however, people are wrongly identified in a spiritual gift, or not released to mature in a spiritual gift, then they are not yet operating at the level that they have been called to. Every child of God needs nurturing to reach their full potential in God. He Heals, He ordains, He commissions, He anoints.

The Levite priests were called to confirm those claiming that they were healed. The elders had the authority to lay hands and pray for the sick and also establish authenticity on those who identified that they carried Gods spirit and authority.

The Bible unveils in 1 Corinthian 14:32 that *the (Spirit) of Prophets is subject to the prophets*. As people mature in their gifting's, they are qualified to authorize and release others at various levels.

To mentor, to grow and become Elders. Not referring 'Elder' as an old person but to the mature in Christ.

The Bible teaches that we should leave an inheritance for he next generation because each generation is required and designed to achieve even more than the last. We should submit to our leaders with grace, humility and love, to then finally be released to lead others, with Honor and understanding of the anointing (ability) that we have been given.

The spiritual power that activates a gift is called a mantle. If people's gifts are wrongly identified then they sometimes fail to develop under the mantle for the type of anointing that they carry. Even more importantly, some spiritual gifts require a certain mantle to activate them. Without it, fullness is not achieved and the gift remains dormant.

People develop into their spiritual giftings, it is important that they are released and encouraged to function in the gifts that God has given them. There should be evidence by signs of spiritual maturity and evidence of spiritual fruit. This is then confirmation that they have developed from 'Gift' status to 'Office', status. If someone has the Office of any of the five-fold gifts, then it means that they operate strongly in that gift.

We are capable of having more than one gift. 1 Corinthians 14:1 says, *Earnestly desire the gifts of the spirit, especially the gift of prophecy.*

It amazes me that many fail to understand the prophetic gifts, yet they have the ability to see and read these texts at will. There has been a short circuit in the body of Christ whenever, there is adverse talk of the five-fold ministry. That is the reason why we fail to see an abundance of power activated through the Church.

Although there are prophetic encounters and training. The Apostolic office is not obsolete. It needs to be taught, activated and imparted. Once the five-fold gifts are identified in a ministry and fruit is evident, then affirming commissioning should be done to establish a person into their 'office'.

The commissioning speeds up their growth and development and releases and activates an ability in their mantle to achieve more than they have ever seen previously. It's a supernatural impartation to 'finish' the mandate they have been given by the Holy Spirit.

However, those commissioned need spiritual covering and accountability as their character is continually shaped and tested.

They need mentoring Apostle's who will help them achieve the hidden things of our own nature that we cannot see. The mentors will usually be able to guide and teach and encourage them.

Some pastors may not know or even recognize prophetic gifts, simply because he/she is not prophetic and cannot identify the prophetic offices in the spirit. Amos 3:7 says that *God does nothing without first showing the Prophets.* It also says that the church was built on the doctrine of the Apostles and Prophets.Therefore, if a prophet or Apostle identifies a five-fold Gift, on someone, they will want to commission or (call out and endorse) the gift, even if it is lying dormant. This work is done in the spirit.

Commissioning confirms the gift on a person's life with heaven. It is a heavenly covenant. This is not to be confused with Ordination. Ordination is for the specific work in the Church ministry, to be carried out by that Church Leader.

A commissioned five-fold minister will be a great benefit to any Church or denomination as they are to work with those leaders to bring the Church into a fruitful position. The five-fold ministry is not denominational rather scriptural.

Five-fold ministry is Gods template for growth, order and a structure where people will grow and thrive, in or out of the building. There can be controversy with understanding the Spiritual gifts, for example, if someone can have a seer gift but not flow prophetically. Even though the seer gift is in itself prophetic by nature, they will have to develop their prophetic gift despite being able to see supernaturally.

There are elements to the prophetic ministry that needs deeper understanding than just the surface function of the gift. This is why the Apostles and teachers need to be activated to bring clarity and teach the full functions of the five-fold ministry gifts.

Ephesians 4:12, explains that spiritual gifts are bestowed to equip his people for works of service, so that they body of Christ may be built up. In other words, we need to be trained up how to use our power.

When Jesus was baptized by John, usual protocol was broken to ensure that Jesus achieved His baptism. John remarked to Jesus, that he was not good enough to baptize Jesus, it should be the other way round, as Jesus already walked in the full authority of his gifts. However, God allowed this and Jesus replied in response to John's caution, 'let it be so for now'!.

Jesus was in the full understanding that he too, needed to be endorsed in the same way we do today with baptism and commissioning by another servant of God, to activate our God given gifts. Immediately after Jesus was Baptized, the Holy spirit came upon him (Power) in the symbol of a dove and God declared that 'He was well pleased', in His Son.

There was a spiritual acknowledgement of this commissioning. There was no limitation on Johns authority to carry out this act. God sent a sign of his approval and immediately, once he was baptized, Jesus was brought into the wilderness (A place untouched by human hand) by the enemy and to test his authority.

Jesus was tempted in the wilderness to (touch the untouched by turning stones into bread, as he was hungry, not thirsty) This was against the principal of God, therefore Jesus declared and reestablished a reminding principal to satan, that '*Man shall not live by bread alone*'. His mantle was challenged yet activated by self control and stewardship of the word, maintaining His authority. The enemy will challenge us through the power of suggestion!

In the Garden of Eden, the serpent tempted Eve, saying, '*Surely you shall NOT die*' despite God saying that eating of a certain fruit would result in spiritual death.

We must know the word of God and guard our salvation from subtle temptations and alternations of it, lest we sell our own soul for promises. The enemy of our lives will always have suggestions of popularity, money and fame and luxury as a bargaining tool in exchange for access to our soul.

When the Apostles were commissioned they distributed evenly all that they had amongst them and followed Jesus. God's power and sustainability was enough. They understood that the Kingdom walk with Jesus at the level of authority that they had been granted was not about what they owned. It was about what they had to Give! The spiritual gift of Apostleship enables the bearer to be hugely sacrificial giving anything of His own possessions, even His life, to fulfill the mandate of God.

When God called me, He said, "*Give away your Mercedes Benz!*" I obeyed! I experienced a burning desire to get it off my land because I knew that holding on to the car, would block my blessings.

When I settled in our first family home in Texas, we were first blessed with a Farm truck and then with a second car to drive long distances for ministry. In the middle of praying and prophesying over a couple one Sunday morning, my husband and I were asked to come outside. As we did, we were given keys and a title to the second car.

We stood amazed, the congregation were joyful because a car had been given away the previous week in the same Church. God's mandate is catching and the anointing rubs off on all of us wherever we are. That is how we affect the believers, by testifying and showing of what God can do in our lives when we follow everything he says we should do.

As a result of successfully passing His test after Baptism, Jesus's authority increased. This was the beginning of His ministry as he defeated satan who suggested that he did not have any authority. When yo have authority, you don't fight for it, you just BE. Jesus said, I AM that IAM.

The devil hates to hear that you know who you are. He will try everything to bring you to doubt or memories of failure, but as long as you stay firm. He will re reduced to function from the sidelines and observe Gods greatness in your life. The Bible says, *when you resist the enemy, he will flee.* This is to tell you that looser's don't hang around for very long.

There is a requirement for people who have spiritual gifts to be commissioned in those gifts so that the gifts can be acknowledged and activated for the benefit of equipping responsible leadership roles into the Church.

A child of God needs to grow and function into his ministry. Pastors need to be supported to grow from shepherding flock to nurturing leaders to be ready to 'go out' and be the Church in the world. Many today do not!

Instead, they enable the weaknesses in people and hold on to people who have the potential to grow strong in Christ. These people, remain seated in pews longer than necessary and hence their maturity is not developed. We then experienced a weakened Church that provides a poor witness of Gods love and Power.

Those who are commissioned and accountable to the five-fold ministry calling will increase in everything they set out to do, and eventually birth His/Her own ministry after a time of nurture by His leader. They will grow as the mantle (anointing matures) and confidence increases, equipping her to release others in this pattern, God will lead the leader.

I have witnessed that some leaders in the Church are intimidated by those who excel above their leadership. They develop deeper relationship with the Holy Spirit and develop their gifts above and beyond what their Pastor could have taught them. God desires for people to be nurtured until they can stand as leaders and become the nurturers.

There is no need for competition. It is one faith, One God. If we know who we are and our function, we can do a better job of empowering each other than competing.

Jesus was criticized for feeding a man on the sabbath. The law of love overrides natural law because although the law says you cannot work on the sabbath. The Law of Jesus's love, petitions us to love based on the 10 commandments; Love your brother as yourself. If a man is hungry and thirsty then you should feed him.

It is the law of Love, that the needs of a man to be fed, despite the law. The law of the Old Testament required tedious and long-winded submission, which if broken required sacrifices and separations from the community. The new covenant replaced that law. Our sincere repentance replaced legal requirements and ensured that we were still in covenant with Jesus, despite our mistakes.

It would be like saying feed the hungry on every day except the Sabbath, simply because feeding represents working. Thus, the man would starve. Jesus's love demonstrates, feeding the man, which no law should stop. The law represents legalism but left no room for compassion. Old Testament law would make the law of love incomplete.

The new covenant on our heart, convicts us to take action, overriding legalism of the Law because Jesus died for our sins, to replace the Law.

Some Churches have not recognized the need to raise up and send leaders into the world with a mandate to 'Go and Grow'. To fulfill scripture in Matthew 16:15 we are to go and preach and teach the Gospel into every nation. We are designed to have an impact in society in one of the 7 Pillars of society each representing our growth as humanity.

The 7 Pillars are Business, Government, Media & Arts, Education, Entertainment, the Family and Religion. We are to include these 7 pillars into the mandate that God has given us. The seven pillars of society require Gods influence and standards to not only form the Kingdom structure but to raise up a generation in any nation to have Kingdom impact. To effectively impact a nation for Jesus Christ, we need to have effective leaders in the seven pillars of society in every country because that's where change for the greater good happens.

As prophetic people are raised up, some will outgrow their leaders and ministries.

As they grow, they will sow back into the ministries that birthed them and nurtured their growth and walk in unity for the equipping of those coming up in the Kingdom. Some have a myopic view and consider a following of people to belong to a man's personal ministry.

The 21st Century Church has been seduced with the wrong motive and intimidate, influence, hold back, bribe and limit Gods people by withholding empowerment. The truth sets you free, truth causes you to grow and be empowered. Truth activates your critical thinking and allows you to grow in the revelation God wants to give you.

When Jesus died on the cross and His work on the cross were finished. The Curtain in the temple was torn from the top down. There would be no more requirement for the High priest to make an annual atonement for the sin of man. Jesus established direct communication, beyond the veil.

Some leaders are scared of releasing people into their calling. They try to control and hold on to people's destinies, often drip feeding them information keeping their vision limited instead of empowering them to grow and instead of duplicating themselves by sharing all thats inside of them into someone else.

Money and power status over people become the priority focus away from the mandate of Christ in its fullest capacity. It is shifted from its original mandate and tries to replace all that is required of God to get His people to where they need to be and how they need to function.

People belong to God and the spiritual gifts he gives are given freely given without repentance to his people for his glory. Our job is to serve Jesus and edify ourselves and others through His commandments so that we can do his work. Forming a body of believers who are mature and active in all the five-fold gifts.

The commandment to subdue the earth as in Genesis forms a template on which to increase our faith and authority. A religious spirit that governs by law in a legalistic manner, does not empower or offer grace or even strive for understanding. This will attract all manner of hindrances to those called to dominate the earth. If we first do not subdue, then we have already placed ourselves beneath the level at which we were designed to function.

Pastors would benefit to partner with prophetic ministries to help raise up the five-fold spiritually gifted in their Churches, regardless of their denomination.

That will prevent those who are prophetically awoken, leaving ministries that they currently attend and becoming desolate in search of a Church that embraces and gives liberty to the five-fold Ministry. Those who have a spiritual awakening, search for their tribe, others who are like they are.

When a Church is immature and not reaping much five-fold harvest, it is a sign that the Church needs a revision of the structure that it functions under. The gifts are for the edification of the Body of Christ. A Church or gathering should grow and impact communities.

If Jesus is coming back for His bride now, then what will he see when the five-fold ministry is absent. Nothing should stay the same and so must we. We must be transformed by the renewing of our minds daily.

Every day we are to be able to shift from old thinking. If we don't renew our minds from what happened yesterday, we will stay in the same place. We will witness others grow spiritually and leave us in the same place of spiritual immaturity and without power.

There are hindering spirits with religious behaviors of control with an agenda that is not of God. The awakening of the prophetic Church is uprising everywhere, enabling God's people to reach their full potential.

No more stagnant, noisy sermons that fail to empower people. These services may entertain, but the true word of God convicts and transforms. It's a serious business and it is life changing.

God's Spirit is Apostolic. I am very passionate about the Apostolic because I am a doer. It is, by nature a very entrepreneurial gift. It pioneers, innovates, solves problems and publishes its templates, as does the Apostle.

The Prophetic represents God's design and ability, and authority to speak and declare a thing into being like an entrepreneur.

The Apostolic represents God's design and structure and authority to execute and produce a thing into the manifestation of abundance.

The five-fold gift of the Apostle, solves problems and can flow through all areas of the five-fold gifts, Prophet, Evangelist, Teacher and Pastor. It simultaneously builds up and plants (Establishes) and tears down what is not required for the benefit of the people, nation or country, with an ease and a grace and ability given by God. Because it is God, it is successful. The Apostle is designed with curiosity to ask, to know and implement successful blueprints from start to finish. The Apostle functions at a high level of Gods commandments, truth and conviction.

The Apostle is given the ability to flow through all the spiritual gifting's, dispensing them as required. Identifying, nurturing and releasing them as needed in the Church as it grows where the gift is accepted and valued and honored.

God takes the honor of the Apostle so seriously that in the Bible he commands that if an Apostle is rejected they are to symbolically wipe their feet as they leave a place that they are called to. All judgment can remain in the place of rejection.

Matthew 10:14 states that w*hosoever shall not receive you, nor hear your words, when ye depart out of that house or city, shake off the dust of your feet.* This implies that if God sends a Prophet to you then it is to warn, to bless or to release his heart to you. If God sends an Apostle to you, it is to get you to your destiny and start, therefore if you reject an Apostle, how can you begin? What is your blueprint?

The Apostle is gifted to attract supernatural provision, the prophetic lifegiving word to release power and favor to start and reach the finish line from the beginning foundational vision.

Apostles are usually at the beginning and pioneering of most things, they are gifted visionaries. Apostles and prophets know how to hear the heart and mind of God for you and bring the revelation to a person a region or a church to transform it.

The burden the Apostle feels for His people is the exact DNA as God. While trying to execute the mandate as best as possible based on the revelation given, the apostle has to respond to the Holy Spirit who will give instruction in the spirit.

The Apostle and prophet will shift quickly to complete tasks, calling on resource, relationships and skill and insight to get the task complete. Many may not understand their methods, their timing and their function. It is supernatural and you will know if they are authentic, by their fruit and the prophetic words they speak coming to pass.

They do not function from a standpoint of gaining permission from man because they are SENT by God and that is how the completion comes. They have an 'unction' that drives them.

Sometimes they function in area where they have never ever functioned, in a skill or gifting. Yet as they in faith, put one foot in front of the other, the Holy Spirit instructs and guides them to complete the task.

The Evangelist has a gatherer's anointing and is great at communicating, networking, and telling people about the Good News of Christ yet carrying a great anointing to bring people together. The Evangelist has a sunny outlook on many circumstances that arise, but yet stays focused on the heart of the people being connected to God at all costs.

Teachers are anointed at discovering Gods secrets and teaching Gods principles, sharing hidden gems and revelation that allow us to tap into our own inheritance. The Teacher can train the next generation on how to achieve Gods best for our lives and develop The Church with understanding and knowledge.

Through arduous study and revelation the teacher scribes God's mind, helping us to understand historical and generational precepts and holding to account our behaviors and growth based on Gods infallible word. The teacher is a thinker and thinks about God continually, asking God to show examples from everyday life's teaching to those that need understanding.

The Bible quotes in Proverbs 4:7, *'Wisdom is the principal thing; therefore, get wisdom: and with all thy getting get understanding.'* When you have the understanding of something, then you can correctly divide truth and discern.

The Pastor, is great at nurturing people, like a spiritual welfare officer who specializes in the wellbeing, professional and personal development of people. The Pastor manages every day matters in the community of the body of Christ and is the shepherd keeping abreast of everyday issues.

The Pastor will also search for resources that will enable people to grow and become more effective in their walk, praying with them and having a day to day relationships with them, looking out for them in a holistic manner. Shepherding Gods mandate and their walk with it.

All five-fold offices are required to go and preach and teach the Gospel in every nation. All can achieve greater levels than they first discovered in Christ through growth and constant devotion and relationship with him.

All five-fold offices need to receive the gift of the Holy Spirit which will empower them to live a fulfilled life in relationship with the father and discover the measure of the authority given to them by God.

This will also empower them to rule and pray over countries, over time, over principalities, to heaven and with dominion over hell, creation and their own lives.

When we subdue the earth, it means everything working in partnership, because we have the legal right to it all. Any other spirit that was not sent to the earth realm by God himself, is illegal and we have authority over any spirit not of God.

Many who have unbelief in Jesus compare religious practices and other beliefs that go against the acknowledgement of the Holy Spirit. Any other spirit is not of God.

God is very clear about what is good for us and any other suggestion no matter how harmless it may seem, if it is not serving God then it is not something that can yield Gods fruit.

There is only one authentic spirit of God. Satan, despite being a talented, good looking worshipper was cast out of heaven into the air because of pride and a puffed up ego. To this day, still uses the same manipulation of the mind to trick us out of being sure that we were called into a relationship with God and that we do actually have complete authority and authenticity.

Satan makes suggestions which play on our minds. Such as ego, pride and thinking we are better than anyone else and belong to an exclusive club because we have a gift or talent or even that we are not yet good enough.

God is not about exclusion. His word say's that we have all fallen short of the glory. By this he is expressing that without Him we are all unworthy, but because of His love, he has made us worthy.

We have already been given the spirit of leadership, to dominate the 7 Pillars of society. The only one who can stop you reaching your goal to be great is YOU. Our lives and destinies are a consequence of the actions we take every day. Every broken and hurting person is yearning for a touch from God. Every happy place is his and every desire and motivation should also be his. Gods will should be our will so that everything we do and put our hearts and minds to, is motivated by what He would want for us.

Our lives should line up with Jesus's 'WILL'.

When we put our trust in God, we are fruitful in whatever we do because it is what he would like for us to be doing.

Without God we end up achieving less than we should have achieved.

"A man's weakness and strength, purity and impurity are his own, and not another mans, they are brought about by himself and not by another; and they can only be altered by himself, never by anyone else. All that he achieves and fails to achieve is the direct result of his own thoughts, actions and mind.'

Quote by James Allen.

Be Transformed By the Renewing Of Your Mind

2 Timothy 1:7 *For God has not given us a spirit of fear, but of power and of love and of a sound mind.*

Philippians 4:13 *I can do all things through Christ who strengthens me.*

Luke 4:18 *The Spirit of the Lord is upon me, because he hath anointed me to preach the gospel to the poor; he hath sent me to heal the brokenhearted, to preach deliverance to the captives, and recovering of sight to the blind, to set at liberty them that are bruised.*

CHAPTER 1 - SAVED TO SERVE

Discussion Points

1. How long can it take to understand who you are and what you are called to do?
2. What does God put in us?
3. How long do your gifts last?
4. Why is forgiveness important?
5. How does the truth set you free?
6. If you are traumatized can truth help?
7. Can anyone be a leader?

Activation

1. What has hindered your thinking?
2. Recite a scripture that empowers you
3. Find a partner and pray encouragement and a blessing to each other
4. Pray the affirming empowerment statement all week;
   'This week I will ask God what my purpose is?

CHAPTER TWO

THE BEAUTY OF ESTHER

Esther was not only beautiful spiritually by being a humble trusting woman, she was obedient to her uncle Mordecai, (An Apostle), He 'SENT' her. She honored his wisdom and his guidance. That made her beautiful inside too.

A woman who can trust is beautiful because she does not act out of fear and does not have the need to control just simply be a graceful woman and allow God to have full authority over her through whom she is sent to serve. She can be trusted. This is Apostolic.

Anytime you see in the Bible a commission or commandment to do something, this is Apostolic. The Apostle is an Ambassador of Christ. One who walks in His same authority. An Ambassador is a high ranking Diplomat.

The country that they originate from is called the 'SENDING' Country. We are Ambassadors of Christ SENT by Christ with the Kingdom of Heaven mandate. Ambassadors have immunity against certain laws in other countries and very many privileges. Wherever we go, we take the Kingdom of God with us. The Bible says, it is AT HAND.

Regardless of what challenges life brought to Esther, she found herself chosen to be in the Kings hareem, set up like many women, beautified and on a waiting list to be one of the Kings brides. It was probably very intimidating with all the other beautiful women called to serve the King, fussing about their appearance and how they can please the King. She followed protocol until her time had come. She trusted her uncle. He had the wisdom of God and it was to save her so that she in turn could save a nation.

What a mandate!

My Esther moment came when I was invited to HRH Prince Charles State Apartments for a business reception. As I looked around the room, the only Black businesswoman in the room. I saw no one that I knew and before I could get acquainted with the audience.

A loud announcement was made, My Lords Ladies and Gentlemen, I present HRH Prince Andrew, Your Highness Yana Johnson. As I looked up startled, lights, cameras and Palace guards were all standing before me as the Prince asked, "Why do our Designers leave the UK?".

I was stunned!

However, something came over me and without training or a Mordecai, I gathered my composure and stood with my shoulders back and out of my mouth the first correct protocol, led by the Holy Spirit of course, I uttered, 'Your Highness'.

Without much effort, I began to share of the industry challenges I faced (in summary of course) and I had identified the answer, because the challenges that I faced, mirrored that of all other startup manufacturers in the UK. I was SENT to deliver my nation. When I paused, the Prince, further questioned me on what should be done about it, and again, I held a plausible solution. However, I am aware that this crossed line of Governmental protocol and he was ushered away to the next guest. I had the Prince captive audience for longer than was allowed.

Esther was able to capture audience with the King for longer than was usually allowed. The King inside of us both demanded His audience.

I was soon after nominated for a Queens Honour MBE (Member of the British Empire) For Services to Cosmetics. I collected my honour in the palace along with my family in 2009 and received a Royal Bow/Pin from HRH Prince Charles.

27 years earlier, my father built a row of 13 houses, pioneering a project which has become a legacy of what Jamaican immigrants achieved. The scheme ACAFESS, was visited by HRH Prince Charles 27 years earlier than when I received my award. God had established something long before it was to be manifested.

Queen Vashti ruled as Queen, yet had dishonored Palace order and had broken protocol in her public dishonor to the King. Her actions angered and embarrassed Him. Her actions forced the King to have her killed, based on her actions. Her behavior resulted in her death as a result of challenging the Kings authority, thus she was no more. He may have been her husband, but He was still The King!

Being married to a prophetic man, I realize that although my husband can benefit from the nurture and wisdom God gives to me, I am also to serve Him as the head of the house, as a Prophet and serve Him as the Apostle and head of our household and of our spiritual lives.

I praise God that I had developed into the identity of who I am as an Apostle, otherwise, I would not have been able to be with the right husband for my destiny, because I would not have known my identity. You cannot choose a spouse based on their looks, wealth or status in life. If you do not connect spiritually the relationship is very hard work. Every marriage has a purpose.

Eddie is my husband, and I honor and respect His office and rank in the Kingdom, because God has given it to him and he respects mine. We both serve God in who we are and what we have to bring to the table individually and collectively.

Proverbs 14:1 warns, that a foolish woman tears down her own household with her mouth therefore, I use the wisdom that God has given to me and petition Him when I need to see changes that concern my husband and I. I don't override him and take it into my own hands.

Vashti, ruled as Queen, but next to the King she needed to allow Him to lead. To bring grace and honor to her life. However, she didn't and her attitude and decisions, cost her, her life. Esther also disobeyed Palace rules by entering the Kings courts without invitation. However, her attitude was different, she was meek and humble. She was shrouded in God's grace, acting in a place of pure self sacrifice with a greater purpose for the good of her nation. She attracted the favor of God. Her response no matter how disobedient, was not selfish. This was an act of Love which overided the Law.

God backed her up, she did not perish because her motive was not self-serving. She had a greater mandate at hand and had won favor of the King who trusted her. He was intrigued by her and he wanted to serve her. When you have demonstrated humility to a man, God will use Him to serve you. He will protect you and please you. You will be happy.

Esther, knew that her fete was covered in risk, there was no assurance that the King would accept her dramatic entrance, she knew this. Those around her asked her if she knew what she was doing and challenged her with a stream of 'What if's?' to which Esther famously replied, '*If I perish, I perish!*', she was not haughty or arrogant. She was sturdy and set in God. Her Apostolic grace to achieve Mighty Works was activated.

She put her own life on the line to make a plea, knowing full well this could have been her last entrance resulting in death. The King would not be embarrassed again by a woman who would potentially undermine Him. The Palace courts would not tolerate such a repeat of dishonor. It could have been a disaster for Esther. She gambled everything she had. The stakes were very high, but he was The King and he loved her and she was SENT.

The King had however, observed her humility and he sought to protect her from the wrath of the Palace Law. When Esther entered His courts without invitation, breaking protocol, he quickly (even by the surprise of Esther) stretched out his scepter just in time to receive her and make her entrance a legal one. He pretended to know of her audience, and acted as if he expected her. Esther was unannounced and uninvited into His courts. Such an entry into the Palace, could have resulted in her death.

Esther's humility saved her life. Her beauty brought grace and favor with the King who protected her against the palace protocol for certain death. The King accepted her entrance into His court and protected her from death which meant that she was now His responsibility. Beauty can be such that women use it to their advantage as Men like to look at beautiful women. Some women use their beauty to manipulate and disguise their motive which is influenced in ungodly gain.

I mentioned in Chapter 1 how hurting people sometimes hurt other people. Misunderstanding and accepting our differences can hinder unity, and create disharmony. Issues of the heart can cause us to have knee jerk reactions and become overly sensitive and insensitive to others, hurting them in the process of protecting our own fears.

Unity in relationships occur where all parties demonstrate humility and love towards each other. It is choosing to get the best result for the common good. It is Honor. Humility attracts peace and love. Humility sustains relationships and smoothes out misunderstandings. Humility is the language of servanthood and ultimately love.

Women are created to be humble, nurturing and loving. We are by design multitaskers. God knew that he created man with a mind to focus on what he had given him to do and sometimes women can feel that a man is selfish in His pursuit of His design.

Ladies, I present to you that Man is simply doing what he was created to do. He is not worrying about his hair, his weight or his shoes. He does not carry the same insecurities as some women. He is very straight down the line instructional and of action. He is designed to be on purpose.

Woman, however, are created in all beauty and splendor to be a help to man. Women have gifts and abilities designed to compliment his weaknesses as well as his strengths. Women are called to know and function from a more detailed stand point.

Being humble is not being weak. Women have been given the same authority as man. Both man and woman were called Adam before the fall! Looking good and feeling good about yourself is a good thing. Balancing your time to nurture your household and your husband and family is also a great asset. Family is the garden that we are all put in to grow.

Women are to grow and reach their highest level in God, so that her identity is rooted in Him and she knows who she is. She knows what she carries and she is aware of her strengths, so that when she meets a man, she is not obsessed in what he thinks of her. She is not weakened by being unsure of who she is next to Him, but rather a strength in her own right and a powerhouse of love to the man who needs to be celebrated by her for all that he does, for who he is.

Learning to be the best you, prepares you for marriage and great relationships where you can bring the best of you into the relationship.

Being mature and secure in yourself first before even thinking of a relationship with someone else. If you don't mature then you will not choose your partner wisely. You won't be able to!

I have heard and witnessed women writing long lists and being specific about this miracle husband who will be the solution and answer to all things. Some women want men that wouldn't even match who they are. They have this idea that the man will fix everything about them and complete them.

I come to bring truth that we MUST do the inner healing, the identity work in Christ and the character building before we present ourselves as a mate to someone else. Otherwise the procedure will be done in the process of relationship which can be messy and create long lasting hurts to both parties which take time to heal instead of just enjoying the relationship. The secret to finding a great husband is to heal yourself. You will attract what you are. Do the personal work to grow and mature so that when you meet him, you are equally as desirable to be with. As a woman thinketh so she is!

Marriage is for Gods purpose as well as our own desires being matched in that covenant. However, taking responsibility for what we have to offer someone else, will prepare you to have something to bring to the table in the relationship. You should be able to stand on your own two feet if required.

God is your strength not man!

You marry man, not the anointing! You serve each other!

God is your provision when man fails or gets it wrong. God should be your first love. That way he can set the template for you to have a standard to uphold for your life, to match up to His standard and expectation. To be a help and bring something in addition to who your spouse is in the relationship.

God's standards for your life is designed to help you reach your own personal potential and govern your direction in life, leading to your success. A praying man will also find his standard and together you will both flourish when you continually pull on God for direction. If your previous relationships have been off track then it is evidence that you are replicating elements of the relationship that you have with God, it is a mirror reflection. It is a guide for you to draw closer to God so that you reflect Him.

No man or woman should ever replace God in our lives, we must first be whole with him to be successfully whole with each other.

A woman has the ability to dominate a boardroom or predominantly male space, just by her presence without having to wear trousers, shout or bully anyone. Having quiet confidence, knowledge, insight, and the gift inside gives an advantage to discern and see a holistic solution to many challenges in business or ministry and life.

Women do not have to compromise their design to be powerful. God created them just as they are to be complete in what they have to bring to the table. The enemy uses insecurities of image to prevent woman functioning in her full design. Women make great partners and keep a man grounded. Striving for too much power, money or possessions is a warning of imbalance, however. Women like to acquire nice things, so being career minded and independent is never wrong as long as balance is applied.

A woman is an asset to a business and marketplace ministry and a gem in the family. The woman in Proverbs 31:10 is not only industrious, but knows how to strike a balance, so that her husband trusts all that she does and is not intimidated by her.

A true woman of God like Esther will be humble, meek, a great communicator and keen to know what pleases a man BEFORE herself so that she can fulfill her design and help him.

71

When she has become a trusted person in His life and consistent in her own heart, it will show on the outside and she will have not only his attention but his heart and protection.

A man's covering is a huge grace God gives to a woman. The world has perverted it and released songs that empower the need to berate and belittle the need for the right man in our lives. These songs are a lie of the enemy.

In 1 Peter 3:6 the Bible says, *even as Sara obeyed Abraham, calling him lord: whose daughters ye are, as long as ye do well, and are not afraid with any amazement.*

Humble confidence in a woman is attractive to a man. When he pursues you out of this attraction he will respect you and work hard to honor your relationship.

I once said to my husband that I'm a Princess, and that he was my Prince. He replied, 'No you are a Queen', and I looked at Him and asked 'Why?'', because really, I wanted to be a Princess. He replied, 'Because Princesses, don't rule!'.

So many times, we idolize movies and take on the princess role thinking that Prince charming is promised to each of us, when in fact, we have been given the authority to dominate as Kings and Queens, under the mantle of our King Jesus, who made us in his image.

When you flow in the maturity and grace of God. You will have others wanting to sit under your mentorship, help you and support your tasks in business, work or ministry. Esther had a mutual friend, a Eunuch who knew what the King liked, he prepared her to stand out. He was a great friend to her destiny.

Men don't want to be challenged by a woman who is a know-it-all. This threatens his design to lead. Men want to be encouraged and supported, needing help only which they ask for. Men come to you for help when they need you.

It is through this beautiful attitude that you, a woman will attract his heart especially if you can be vulnerable. When he witnesses you being vulnerable He will jump at the challenge to fix things and take care of you and cherish you. That is man's design.

If he has hurt you himself and recognizes through your clear communication motivated in love, forgiveness and understanding then he will listen to you and ask for help to do better and protect you. Your humility will impact change in him. Projecting you fears, insecurities and weaknesses on a man pushes Him away.

Your humility will impact change on anyone if it is sincere. We learn from Esther, that Humility is POWER. Jesus was humble throughout all of his life and most of all during his persecution and he laid down his life, choosing not to defend himself but to allow the WILL of the father to be completed through him.

If your man is a good provider or works in a servant leader capacity where he is sent to nurture others, He may not have the time for what you imagined. He will be busy and in demand. You will need to be patient and allow him to fulfill his design and support him.   Learn to share Him in the grace of God.

He is on purpose with God's call on his life, hence your petition is with God for all the issues that arise concerning what you want and what you don't want. You reach a man's heart by praying to God, not nagging him.

To stay beautiful and wrinkle free, to attract people to your life and to have Gods chosen man for you yearning for your love and attention, is to pray into everything that would otherwise cause frustration in a relationship. Pray without ceasing, over everything. Anything not showered in prayer is subject to an attack from the enemy.

God is your preservation and your defender. He is your provider, so let him provide his best for your life. The match he has for you is better than if you choose yourself.

Marriage is a ministry, therefore when you know your purpose, even dating takes on another meaning, because you will choose wisely. I don't believe in Girlfriends and Boyfriends in the Kingdom of God, they should be Husbands and Wives. The dating experience and agenda has an expiry date on it and without the true focus to learn someone's character with the intention of marriage, and servanthood, defilement and lust creeps in through the 'dating' process resulting in unnecessary soul ties and disappointments.

In choosing your future destiny helper, husband or wife, you will choose according to the tasks you have ahead and the life that has been developed for your purpose. Random dating distracts the focus from your purpose if not focused on the purpose of the union it is intended to create.

When I was single, I would pray, God send me someone who is doing what i'm doing, which at the time was as a traveling Apostle, preaching, praying and teaching in conferences or in a home setting, literally wherever I went.

You will be matched according to your purpose and the need you have to fulfill it. God will design the man who matches your calling on these areas which fulfills both of your purposes. You will eventually become one, synchronizing at the beginning creates harmony as your relationship grows.

Staying married and in love can be challenging when people have ulterior motives and hidden agendas. Sometimes they are not fully healed and want to escape the refining process in a relationship, blaming the other person. God sends us people who will agitate us to grow and develop a higher spiritual mentality. They rub us up the wrong way and cause some challenges, but until we learn to subdue the attitude and aggression in our own character, we are still babes very capable of creating a big mess every time we try a new relationship.

The role people play in our lives challenges us and tests our character which causes us to have to address our own development and thus grow closer in a relationship with God.

God wants us to stay beautiful in prayer, expose and reveal the motive of our hearts. We shouldn't be fighting or displaying ugliness as Kingdom children, the fruits of the spirit are; Love, joy, peace, patience, kindness, meekness, self-control, longsuffering, gentleness.

This is the oil of beauty, not even your heart should be troubled when you reach a certain place in God. Remembering that only he can truly give and take away. For our own good, He desires for us to become flexible so that he can maneuver us into our full destiny.

We should strive to display a beautiful character which attracts all the things we need to move ahead and excel, to network and to have successful relationships, friendships, jobs, ministries and communities.

It is that light that shines through us developed by Jesus Christ to enlighten, love and be an example to others to also know him and His life changing power.

Psalm 46:10 declares, *"Be still and know that I am God!"*

You are beautiful. You were born beautiful created in Gods image.

Be Transformed By the Renewing Of Your Mind

Matthew 11:28 *Come all ye who are burdened and heavy laden and I will give you rest.*

Isaiah 61:3 *Appoint unto them that mourn in Zion, to give unto them beauty for ashes, the oil of joy for mourning, the garment of praise for the spirit of heaviness; that they might be called trees of righteousness, the planting of the Lord, that he might be glorified.*

CHAPTER 2 - BEAUTY

Discussion Points

1. *How can you be beautiful inside?*

2. *What is Apostolic?*

3. *Give examples of being challenged to be humble, nurturing and loving*

4. *Why do we need inner healing?*

5. *Why is always staying prayer important?*

Activation

1. *How do you like to feel beautiful?*

2. *Share a scripture that empowers you*

3. *Find a partner and pray encouragement and a blessing to each other*

4. *Pray the affirming empowerment statement all week;*

'This week I will feel beautiful by telling someone their qualities'

CHAPTER THREE

THE WISDOM OF QUEENS DEBORAH & SHEBA

*I*n the story of Deborah, we see her as a judge and ruler settling disputes. A Prophet and leader of her time. Deborah's job would not be to fight but as she was the Prophetic leader similar to a ruling King. Her job would be to sing encouraging war declarations and a victory song. The Spirit of God would be attracted to the music she sang as a worship intercessor and descend on the war at hand. She was a prophetic minstrel, so that the song of the Lord would go before her and many battles were won because of her prophetic declarations.

Deborah had the wisdom to handle the office she was called to as well as use her prophetic gifting's in war. She was friends with the sons of Issachar who were very well clued up on where and when things happen based on their Prophetic gifts and discernment of time.

Deborah by association had more gifts that the Bible records. This gave her an advantage, to settle scores amicably with the people whom she was called to judge over in her ruling. Deborah had confidence and knew the timings and judgements and decisions she made were good.

This qualified her as a wise woman.

I believe she was a 'Son'. In other words, she had achieved (Sonship) maturity in Christ, although a woman. God wants us to become mature in Him

The Bible says in Proverbs 16:18, '*Your gift makes way for you, and brings you before great men*'. A very simple statement that has different translations, such as the creative gift or talent that you carry opening doors as people request you in their audience, employment or to enjoy your gift or talent.

Or the present or gift you buy or bring to someones house or business can also open doors for you as alliances are made. The gift makes a good impression of charity, friendship and love. A gift represents thoughtfulness and blessing. If you attend a house with a rather large bunch of flowers, you are likely to receive great hospitality from your host because you have chosen to love and honor them with a beautiful gift.

This goes without saying if you are wise, wisdom will show you where to sow your gift and whom to bless your talent with.

Those who are open minded will create opportunities for your advancement however, those who covet your gifts and are small minded will hide you under a bush or keep you to themselves only. Some even wanting to control your gift.

People can be jealous of your gift and being anointed can sometimes trigger jealousy in others. However, we are to guard our gifts, guard our hearts so that we can always function to be of full effect in our calling. I believe that the word guard means to 'be aware' of who you share your dreams and visions with. Dreaming with dreamers who will encourage and push you to achieve great things. Staying clear of people who do not understand your mandate and who might discourage you and put you off altogether. Or those who are simply jealous of what you carry and the grace you walk in. You can create opportunities of open doors, by having a genuine servant's heart. Servant Leadership is a desired quality to have. Servant leaders have access to people, resources and the favor of the Lord on their life because they have your best interests in their hearts and people warm to their friendly generous character.

Servants obtain great authority from God because like Jesus, they serve others with a loving heart and demonstrate true love. In Chapter 1, we addressed when people are in a broken state and the extremes that they may go to find love and acceptance. The man pleasing spirit, despite the spiritual gifts a person carries, leads them to search for acceptance and validation and become a man pleaser, often giving their gifts where they are not honored, just to hear the voice of a man stroking their ego.

A man pleasing spirit listens to the voice of man above and beyond what God is calling her to do and misses her potential to grow and discover Gods restoration to bring her to a fuller life and place in God.

A gifted person can never reach their potential if they carry a man pleasing spirit as it limits their own effectiveness and presents them from growing higher in a personal relationship with God.

I recently began to teach this to an international group of Pastors, through the invitation of a groundbreaking event. Challenging them to sow/ tithe their time and gifting's as well as paying their own costs to attend an International Conference. Prophetic Global 2016. It was the first Big mandate God had ever given me. I had never held a conference prior and I had to follow the leading of the Holy Spirit for daily instruction.

God told me that the people would be blessed and receive the prophet's reward because they were sacrificial of themselves, serving the vision in another nation.

The international speakers would normally receive payment to travel and minister internationally. However, God wanted to show them that without the normal resources handed to them, He was still their God and can do great miracles, and He did.

Those who caught the vision, felt God all over it because they knew that they had not been challenged to make such a huge sacrifice. This broke them out of their comfort zone and broke off the spirit of limitation from their mindsets.

Prophetic Global 2016 in London was the first in its region of a Prophetic nature. Over 350 people attended and there were manifestations of Diamonds, Gold dust, Healings and uncommon Miracles of provision of food and vehicles for the delegate from the start of the 3 day conference to the last. There are still amazing testimonies of breakthrough from those who sowed of their time in attending.

God proved to all who attended and all who heard about it afterward, that if you extend what you have to those who do not have anything, not only will more come to you, but it will continue to keep coming. When you come into a personal relationship with Jesus, you will attract what you need. It will break you into new places, to meet new people and do things on a different level.

This is where your increase comes from. As you are increased there is more work to do. *'To whom much is given, much is required.'* This is growth and preparation into leadership. Many will not understand. Many may have something to say, but if it was a vision given to you by God, then pursue it.

The Bible says God loves a cheerful giver and some have used this phrase out of context to intimidate giving more than you have and convicting people to feel guilty for not doing so.

Giving in wisdom, giving your time, your love, your encouragement being available for someone else, and listening to people. Wisdom is Gods heart. When you give wisely, you attract people, you attract help and you attract wealth.

If you give unwisely or over give (unwisely), then you can reverse the blessing and cause a curse to come on you. If you enable (Enslave) someone to become dependent on what you give, when they could otherwise provide for themselves. You are generating a slothful spirit. Wisdom in giving is very necessary. God wants us to EMPOWER, not to ENABLE.

The wisest man in the bible was King Solomon. Queen Sheba heard about King Solomon and sought to see him. The bible says that the whole earth sought to have audience with Solomon, so she decided to take a trip to visit him.

She brought 'good' gifts which caused him in return to be an amazing host and give of his time mentoring her while she gleaned of his wisdom, success Blueprints and strategies. Her giving was tangible 'HONOR', in gift form.

Your breakthrough is in giving and in your humility and Wisdom. Everything you want and need externally is within you, but you have to tap into the gifts inside you, develop your relationship with God and access the ability to do these things through those whom he sends into your life. As opportunities open up to you God will give you the insight to understand what he wants and when he wants it.

When you meet someone, ask God, 'What is the purpose that I have met them?', 'How can I impact their life?'. Not 'What can I get out of them?'. This approach usually builds a mutual interest and a genuine alliance in a spirit of servanthood.

Once you have tapped into these principles of how to build and sustain healthy respectable relationships, you begin to attract many things into your life. A lot of people want something free. Free means take what you get, any condition and when it fails to do what it was sent to do don't complain.

Jesus is free to us. However, He is free because he was a sacrifice for us. He paid the price for our sins so that we could receive life ready for us to receive. So, receiving Jesus FREELY has in fact a great value. When the world gives free, there are strings attached and conditions to be met.

Be prepared to pay a price further down the line. If we can be bought with money then we are a slave to it and it will dominate the motivation of our hearts and our minds.

If we can function, knowing that although there is a need, that money can provide a solution to, our faith can stretch further to see God provision to the solution without ever having to find that money.

He can move someone's heart to blessing us with what we need. Kingdom resources is just that! Any heaven sent provision that solves the problem or need.

Money is just one of the Kingdom of Heavens resources.

Faith, love, charity, prayers, blessing, patience, are all resources that when applied to spiritual life become currency. When you activate the faith within you, the impossible begins to happen and you honestly earn and accumulate the things you want in your life, in balance and harmony with a good character and a generous spirit.

I have heard the testimonies of many people who speak of riches accumulated without the power of God. It ultimately leads to destruction as they had no balance in their lives. They acquired the promises of riches but they were empty because there was NO purpose for their abundance.

The Bible says in Mark 10.25, that it is easier for a camel to pass through the eye of a needle than a rich man to enter the gates of heaven, why? Because the rich man has a hard time letting go of the riches.

The eye of a needle is in fact a very small gate that a camel would struggle to go through with his humps, but eventually he would pass through, where the rich man would still be considering his wealth and his comfort and not want to change, the camel would have long gone through the gate and about his journey.

In Matthew 4:4: Jesus answered the temptation of the devil saying, *'It is written, that man shall not live by bread alone, but by every word of God'.* Then Satan took Jesus up on a mountain after his Baptism, the Devil promised Jesus all the land and riches but Jesus knew that all those promises could not satisfy him. Only Gods word and purpose over what we have acquire sustains it.

We need to be humbled by God and delivered from being wasteful, arrogant and boastful instead we should be generous, kind and balanced with what we have. Then we understand and recognize, that man shall not live by bread alone, but by God and His spirit that guides us to live a balanced righteous life. Our resources, our time, our possessions are from the Kingdom and when used for the Kingdom, multiply. It is there that increase happens.

We should remember that there is an entire world to impact, using Gods wealth & time & love to bring solutions to many social and community problems.

Wisdom is about balance.

It's about the motive of the heart and it's about thinking with the mind of Christ. If we are to pursue the 7 Pillars of society and have impact in those places where we can dominate like a King or Queen, then it is Gods wisdom that will get us there and sustain us there.

Queen Sheba was very beautiful and not only did she enter the Kings presence with her beauty but she left with the Kings influence. Let God be the Kings influence on your life.

Being wise is when you know the answer but wait until it's time to speak. Knowing when to take on a battle or challenge. Immature people blurt everything out because they have not yet learned timing and sometimes speak to soon causing offense. Speaking too soon without thinking of the implications of what we say causes offense.

A wise man speaks very little and listens much. In listening you are armed with every bit of information you need and can gather to accurately speak and respond. Knowing in your own heart your strengths and core beliefs.

Not every argument needs to be won on a point. The driving principle of truth can settle a matter in your heart without conflict. Because God is still God and if His word says it then it is so.

When you know who you are, you can have the capacity to learn but still hold on to the principles on which you believe without taking offense to someone else's difference of opinion.

The question you can use to challenge those who challenge you is, '*What is the motive?*'. In negative conflict, you can ask, 'What is the spirit?'.

You are wise. All your life experiences have given you wisdom! Tap into it!

Be Transformed by the Renewing Of Your Mind

1 Corinthians 13 *If I speak in the tongues of men or of angels, but do not have love, I am only a resounding gong or a clanging cymbal.*

If I have the gift of prophecy and can fathom all mysteries and all knowledge, and if I have a faith that can move mountains, but do not have love, I am nothing. If I give all I possess to the poor and give over my body to hardship that I may boast, but do not have love, I gain nothing.

Love is patient, love is kind, it does not envy, it does not boast, it is not proud. It does not dishonor others, it is not self-seeking, it is not easily angered, it keeps no record of wrongs. Love does not delight in evil but rejoices with the truth. it always protects, always trusts, always hopes, always perseveres.

CHAPTER 3 - WISDOM

Discussion Points

1. *Why was Deborah a wise woman?*

2. *Discuss, To whom much is given, much is required.*

3. *How can we use wisdom better in our lives?*

4. *What are other Kingdom currencies?*

5. *Read 1 Corinthians 13*

6. *Why do we need love?*

Activation

1. *What would you do if you were a Queen?*

2. *Recite a scripture that empowers you*

3. *Find a partner and pray encouragement and a blessing to each other*

4. *Pray the affirming empowerment statement all week;*

'This week I will Rule and Reign in wisdom'

CHAPTER FOUR

OVERCOMING THE CONTROL OF JEZEBEL

*W*hen we do anything using intentional charm, manipulation or control this is the spirit of Jezebel that is in operation. The spirit of Jezebel is very powerful in the art of suggestion. Subtle shifts happen because the motive behind the charm and suggestion is not of a pure motive but still effective in its gain.

The spirit of Jezebel is not limited to a woman, it can be seen active in men and women, it is a spirit that dominates and has its own agenda against unity, community and love. Its design, is to stop the advancement of the Kingdom. Supported by lust, greed and power. An unauthorized power that takes matters into its own hands for illegal gain through legal means.

Jezebel is a spirit that creates confusion and controls behind the scenes, often in and through leadership, worship and anywhere that the nurturing process is established to refine people to set them free and see them reach their potential in Christ. Jezebel and his/her wicked agenda creep in to use or misuse power to infiltrate Kingdom maturity in those called to a higher place in God.

The spirit of Jezebel functions to hinder, slow down and create discord dysfunction and stunt the growth and raising up of leaders. Called unto service by God. Strangely enough the Spirit of Jezebel is birthed by fear and then pride and protection. Yet produces more fear in overprotecting and controlling. Jezebel is not interested in people who are already rebellious and have no future because there is nothing to control. They are already doomed.

The Jezebel spirit targets Leadership and those walking in or toward their destiny with a great call on their life and purpose ahead of them. Where a person is rebellious to God, although they are valuable, there is no evidence of God moving in and through their lives, so Jezebel is not attracted to them.

They are also not a threat, therefore the Jezebel spirit has no need to know their motivation because they are not likely to discern her activity or stop it. Dysfunction continues under the radar. Jezebel is content because there is no fruit there.

This is of course a spirit which operates on a spiritual level and activities representing Jezebel in the bible who had an evil agenda and went unchallenged causing many Prophets to die because she was allowed to function unnoticed and through deception captivated and killed Prophets to appease the false God BAAL that she served.

When we serve any God other than Jesus Christ, we empower them and the spirits that serve them. We allow them to become active in our lives by giving them permission to cause havoc and dominate our lives, minds and communities with their ungodly agenda's.

Jezebel uproots, destabilizes, divides and devours love, unity and team efforts. Many times we don't even realize that we have opened the door to these sins and we must overcome them in order to live a full and enriched life.

A Jezebel spirit refuses to admit guilt or wrong, unless it is a temporary admittance of guilt in order to gain "favor" with someone. To accept responsibility would violate the core of insecurity and pride from which it operates. When a Jezebel apologizes it is never in true repentance or acknowledgment of wrongdoing but rather "I'm sorry your feelings were hurt." never really acknowledging their personal responsibility.

This spirit takes credit for everything. While a strong trait of Jezebel is to never take responsibility for his wrong actions or behavior, he also is quick to take credit for benefits for which he contributed no effort.

The Jezebel spirit uses people to accomplish its agenda. The Jezebel spirit lets others do its dirty work. The Jezebel gets another person's emotions stirred up, then lets that person go into a rage. The Jezebel sits back looking innocent, saying, "Who me? What did I do?"

This behavior makes it difficult for even the most ardent truth seekers to pin down exactly what has happened. The Jezebel uses, unauthorized means through authorized people. It's very subtle and causes havoc until discerned.

No one should be angry when we make our own decisions through personal preference on any level.

It is our right to have our own opinion and if someone else is angered by them then watch and discern for the nature of Jezebel rising up.

Jesus loved us so much that he gave us CHOICE. He wanted our love to be so pure that it was tested by us being able to choose Him despite what appeared to be a better option and competed with the Kingdom of God.

The Jezebel spirit is clever in its agenda and withholds information which is a form of control. A Jezebel wields power over you by knowing something you don't know in a situation. In the eyes of a Jezebel, having information you don't have is a powerful weapon of control that the Jezebel stores up and uses later on to spin a web of discord and confusion.

This spirit talks in confusion, it is impossible to converse with a Jezebel in logic. When confronting a Jezebel, the subject may be changed five times in one minute. Confusion keeps them "undiscovered" and unexposed. When you pin down the 'point' and remain on the point any argument is diffused. The points don't even have to be agreed, but by being clear, there is understanding and an exposing of Jezebel.

A Jezebel lies convincingly. No one can lie better than this spirit can. Turning on the charm to make you believe Blue is Red.

He/She always fools those whom he's just met while those who have been victimized by his tactics stand by helplessly.

The ignoring tactic is frequently used when someone doesn't agree with their plans, and they isolate the person by ignoring him forcing them to either "come around" to their way of thinking or be indefinitely ignored. One is not free to disagree with the controller.

A Jezebel will rarely acknowledge another person's actions, not even for something that turned out to greatly benefit the Jezebel. He/she just cannot bring himself to say thank you or to acknowledge that someone else did something right. There is no genuine celebration of others.

He/she never gives credit or shows gratitude, instead criticizes everyone, which is a characteristic of a controller. He/she has to be the one who looks good, so she will quickly sharply criticize anyone who makes a suggestion or plan. Even though he likes the plan, he can only criticise it because the idea did not originate from him. Criticizing others elevates the controller in his own mind.

A person with a Jezebel spirit will always upstage another person. She feels threatened by anyone who dares to steal the limelight or anyone who is a threat to her power and control. If you are with such a person and tell of your accomplishment or victory, you can be assured she will quickly tell of something she has accomplished.

Many people talk habitually, but a Jezebel uses talking as a form of control. In a typical conversation, He/she does all the talking, whether it is about sports, the weather or the Kingdom of God.

Owing to this form of control, she is unable to receive input from anyone in her life. All conversation with her is one sided. You are doing the listening. When a controller is confronted, she commonly spiritualizes the situation, explaining it off on God. This prevents her from owning up to responsibility required of her. The implication is always, "You've got a problem; I don't."

A Jezebel never takes the side of a person in authority, unless it is a temporary action to make herself look good. She often will take credit for someone else's idea. Her main desire is for power and control. There is no conscience when an opportunity for recognition presents itself.

A person with a Jezebel spirit pressures you to do things, seemingly ripping from you your right to choose or make a decision for yourself. She makes others feel as though they don't have enough sense to think for themselves. Those, who operate with a spirit of control also have a clairvoyant spirit. A Jezebel has supernatural help in knowing and sensing information. If she uses this against you, she may say, "I can't tell you how I know this. I just know it." This is not the Holy Spirit, but the help of a clairvoyant or familiar spirit.

Clairvoyance may be defined as the power to perceive things that are out of the range of human senses. Because the Holy Spirit will yield genuine fruitful solutions and scriptural examples to back it up.

Whenever my husband and I give correction we find and use the Godly principle that ministers to the situation in scripture and then have an understanding of how to lovingly address the situation. We have seen a lot of breakthrough as we allow God to minister the truth through His word and not our opinions. We ask, 'What spirit is manifesting in our situation?'. A Jezebel likes to be the centre of attention and doesn't like to see others recognized and applauded. When someone else is recognized, he/she will undermine the person's accomplishments verbally.

Since a Jezebel is never wrong, if you contradict or confront one, get ready to become her worst enemy. As long as you are in agreement with him, all is fine.

But if you confront or challenge her, then look out. You are the target of her fiercest venom. A Jezebel will stop at nothing to destroy your reputation.

A Jezebel spirit is difficult to pin down. If the person is near to being confronted, he or she will skillfully twist the entire situation, trying to make the innocent person look like the one who is attempting to be controlling. As always, the Jezebel will do anything to look like the one who is right. A Jezebel will often imply disapproval to those under his or her control. The controlled person feels no freedom to express an opinion, for fear of disapproval. This can manifest in a marriage or in a working environment, or any environment of hierarchy or unity, even in Church.

A Jezebel is usually blatant regarding his knowledge of everything. Quick to express her opinion in any area, he/she leaves little room for anyone to point out the other side of an issue. He/she has made idols of her opinions.

The Jezebel has strong desire, but all for self. "I want what I want when I want it," describes her worship of self will.

A Jezebel leader will never use the words, *"We have a vision,"* but rather, *"My vision is thus and so"*. No one has room for input in a Jezebel's life. It fraternizes with no one unless it is to get you to "cooperate" with his agenda.

A Jezebel in the local church and is very religious and legalistic but doesn't like authority unless she is in the position of authority. Praying to God and asking forgiveness of any of these traits that have arisen in your life will help you to overcome the spirit of Jezebel that operates in us from a spirit of fear, protection or insecurity.

There are different levels to the narcism that follows the Jezebel behavior. It leaves destruction of the soul wherever it is allowed to function and intimidate. You have the authority to stand up to this manipulative behavior and immobilize its destructive behavior through prayer, repentance and fearlessness. Obeying the Holy Spirit will allow you to acknowledge when He is prompting you to apologize or do something and you will acknowledge your own reactions.

When fear enters your life, it means we have no reliance on God and the Holy Spirit and we take matters into our own hands to achieve a desired result. We do not have the authority to manipulate. Manipulation is NOT of God.

A Jezebel cannot be the only one to have an opinion or desire. When we choose friends, or identify healthy relationships, they should want us to flourish and achieve our potentials if they are to be any good in our lives.

God allows us to freely choose him, therefore we must always operate allowing others in our lives to have free will and love and respect and still be there for them in love in any eventuality.

That is pure unconditional true love. That is how we grow and heal and grow stronger in every situation in our lives. We cannot control people or the outcomes of our own life. We must grow to learn to trust God and allow hurts and emotions to be dealt with by him so that we are free from trying to control everything ourselves.

When we let go and allow God to take control of our lives we cease to argue with people or have expectations that are limiting and crush our spirits. When we learn to put every reliance in God and not in man, our journey in life is much sweeter.

Flexibility, acceptance and respect is your strength to building great relationships!

Be Transformed by the Renewing Of Your Mind

Proverbs 3:5 *Trust in the LORD with all your heart and lean not on your own understanding; in all your ways submit to him, and he will make your paths straight.*

2 Deuteronomy 31:8 *The LORD himself goes before you and will be with you; He will never leave you nor forsake you. Do not be afraid; do not be discouraged.*

Proverbs 11:2 *When pride comes, then comes disgrace, but with humility comes wisdom.*

Luke 17:1-12 *And he said to his disciples, "Temptations to sin are sure to come, but woe to the one through whom they come! It would be better for him if a millstone were hung around his neck and he were cast into the sea than that he should cause one of these little ones to sin. Pay attention to yourselves!*

If your brother sins, rebuke him, and if he repents, forgive him, and if he sins against you seven times in the day, and turns to you seven times, saying, 'I repent,' you must forgive him."

CHAPTER 4 - CONTROL

Discussion Points

1. What is control?

2. What is a controlling spirit?

3. How can we love and forgive even when it's not our fault?

4. What does fear do in your life?

5. What in unconditional love?

Activation

1. What has hindered your unconditional love?

2. List 5 liberties in Christ that he has given you

3. Find a partner and pray encouragement and a blessing to each other over 'the spirit of control'

4. Pray the affirming empowerment statement all week;

'This week I will forgive where I have been controlled'

CHAPTER FIVE

THE LOYALTY OF RUTH

$\mathcal{L}$oyalty is a wonderful thing in life. In our lifetime we meet people and we impact their lives or they impact ours. Some for a reason, some for a season and some for a lifetime. Good relationships are very hard to find and for every relationship that we encounter, there is a purpose that has been designed by God. When I meet someone and a relationship is formed from that friendship encounter, I ask God, what is the purpose for this relationship? He will always show me. Know that there is a tangible reason that they are in my life and that I am in theirs.

Ruth was a Moabite, who married into a Hebrew family of Elimelech and Naomi, whom she met when they left Bethlehem and relocated to Moab due to a famine. Elimelech and his two sons died leaving Naomi and her two daughters-in-law as widows.

When Naomi decided to return to Bethlehem, Ruth decided to go with her despite the fact that Orpah, Naomi's other daughter-in-law went back home. Ruth famously vowed to follow Naomi in the following passage:

"Do not urge me to leave you or to return from following you. For where you go I will go, and where you lodge I will lodge. Your people shall be my people, and your God my God. Where you die I will die, and there will I be buried, May the LORD do so to me and more also if anything but death parts me from you" (Ruth 1:16-17).

This passage is touching. It demonstrates Ruth's ability to accept, take on and submit to the new changes in her life and whatever came with it. Not needing to control anything, but to have trust as a child.

There is a submissive trusting relationship to her Mother-in-Law. I see her unspoken character as a wise, noble woman who understands protocol and knows whats best. Ruth taps into this. All the women mentioned in these Chapters worked in their strength. Humility, honor and grace.

In our families and lives there is often a matriarchal or patriarchal figure sent or raised up in that family that frees us from oppression or the destruction that familiarity plays as an agent of hinderance on our calling.

I have noticed that there is usually at least one family member or family friend, who truly see's all your colors and God uses them as a 'safe' place to help you, rescue you or reveal your purpose that may be hindered by bloodline curses that stop you growing or reaching your full potential. Someone who means good for you and you can trust them. This was the relationship with Ruth and Naomi.

When we ask God for blessings in our life we must accept that he will grant us the desires of our heart but also there will be changes that come with the blessings. In Habakuk 2:2 it says that *we should write the vision and make it plain*, which means identify everything we can think of when petitioning God to go about something with as much detail as we know and pray into it so that God can bless us. Often, we are general and vague and ask, "Lord bless me with a big house',

Then when we get the big house, we had not planned for expensive heating bills in the colder months and the costly repairs to a big house. When you ask for a handsome man, had you considered that the Lord will grant your hearts desires. However, not only your eyes will notice him. Or when you ask for a high performance car, the maintenance bill will be very high because repairs on fast cars is expensive.

You will need to constantly be in prayer to understand the heart and mind of God so that you ask for the right thing for the right reason. Being loyal to God is about always wanting what he wants for you. This keeps you consistent with His will. But also develops loyalty within you.

Many times things will come across our paths that entice us to do something else, maybe you visit a Church and hear worship better than where you currently attend, or it appears that living in a certain area is far better than where you are. The enemy will always try to make things appear that the grass is Greener on the other side of the road. When in fact on every side of the road there are struggles, bills and responsibilities that need to be taken care of.

We have been empowered to change the environment we live in. It shouldn't matter where we are, the light of God should allow the environment we are in to change. The true definition for loyalty is God. Even if we are faithless, He remains faithful. If a believer fails, God will remain loyal.

Many people just mouth loyalty, but it's not a reality in their life. We hear so many people making wedding vows just to get divorced in the end of what was designed to be a fruitful married life and people stop being best friends with someone because they have nothing to offer them anymore.

Being loyal to the word of God, the Mandate of God and the Heart of God will ensure that no matter what presents itself before you, you don't change to achieve it, or receive it, you remain loyal. When you become a woman of loyalty, you also become a woman known for integrity, substance and known for good character.

This banner goes before you and touches Gods heart, because he can see that you will not waiver, you can be trusted with the gifts, mind and heart of God and he increases you from this beautiful character that you have become.

It is not at all easy because many times we are tested and there are always easier ways of doing things, but when you are loyal to Gods character, his nature begins to shine through you and people, opportunities and blessings are attracted to your life. True loyalty never ends. Doubt and fear can accomplish nothing. Loyalty will mature you and build lasting relationships!

Be Transformed By the Renewing Of Your Mind

Proverbs 3:13 *Never let go of loyalty and faithfulness. Tie them around your neck; write them on your heart. If you do this, both God and people will be pleased with you. Trust in the Lord with all your heart. Never rely on what you think you know.*

Remember the Lord in everything you do, and he will show you the right way. Never let yourself think that you are wiser than you are; simply obey the Lord and refuse wrong.

If you do, it will be like good medicine, healing your wounds and easing your pains. Honor the Lord by making him an offering from the best of all that your land produces.

If you do, your barns will be filled with grain, and you will have too much wine to store it all. My child, when the Lord corrects you, pay close attention and take it as a warning.

The Lord corrects those he loves, as parents correct a child of whom they are proud. Happy is anyone who becomes wise who comes to have understanding.

Duet 31:6 Be strong and courageous. Do not be afraid or terrified because of them, for the Lord your God goes with you; he will never leave you nor forsake you."

CHAPTER 5 - LOYALTY

Discussion Points

1. What was special about Ruth?

2. How hard is it to accept change in your life?

3. How can we feel empowered when we have to make big changes?

4. How can we be loyal to God?

5. What can we do if we feel afraid or alone and vulnerable?

6. Where can we find courage?

Activation

1. What has hindered your thinking about loyalty?

2. Recite a scripture that empowers you

3. Find a partner and pray encouragement and a blessing
    to each other over loyalty and overcoming fear

4. Pray the affirming empowerment statement all week;

'This week I will practice loyalty even when its hard'

CHAPTER SIX

THE SERVANTHOOD OF MARY

*H*aving a deep passion for missions, I have seen first hand what the power of servanthood can do when you are sent into a country to meet people whom you have never met and who desire to know you. A stranger who has a heart for them, who has travelled the land far and near to be able to sit and share with them. Regardless of your position or status in life, to love and serve another human being is the single most Godly thing you can do.

In the 10 Commandments it says, '*Love your brother as yourself*', You cannot give what you do not have. In giving what you have, you are not depleted but INCREASED. When you give from a heart that is submitted to God, you are increased. He ensures to replace and give you more than you had to start with.

In the Bible Jesus entrusts the Apostles to go out preaching, sharing and teaching Gods word. He commands that they take nothing with them, no money, bags or purses. He wanted them to experience His divine provision.

Telling them to go from house to house and share of Gods Kingdom, if they accept you, receive whatever they give to you to bless the house, if they reject you, don't take the burden with you, leave and wipe your feet on the way out disconnecting the blessing you had intended to leave with them. Because if they cannot accept Gods servant they do not accept God. When you are rejected, learn to walk away with grace. God doesn't want you to be dishonored, he does great things through honor.

This was like a test, but when you are kind and serve someone and they are ungrateful or then misuse or mistreat you, God has said that this, they do also unto to Him. He is saying, don't even worry about it, because that is also what he went through. If we are his servants, then we will go through persecution too.

Jesus is our protector and defender therefore we do not need to retaliate but rather pray our petition to him and he will heal our hearts and give us more to continue to give.

He gives us the grace not to suffer rejection or hurt but to pass that part unto Him and continue, because there will be some people who have waited all their lives for a touch from God that will move through you.

When we are strengthened in spirit and truth, we become above offense and will not be easily offended as we realize that some people have stony hearts and need to see our Love and charity on a consistent level in their lives for them to open up to the spirit of God. They need to see God in us, and they will test it, just by observing us.

God's great commission has SENT us to win the lost. He said that because he has allowed the tares (weeds) to grow with the Wheat (harvest) there will be some that are harvested for good use and some that are not. That is not of our concern, when we are focused on the result God has designed in us we will be tested along with those who are not His. It will be evident of those who are His and those who are not.

The Bible says in Jeremiah 23, God has a plan of good and not evil, to give you an expected end. (A successful good ending). It is on the threshing floor, (his processing in humility and repentance) that brings us to the glory in God. Overcoming challenges, family discord, forgiveness, Joy and Dunamis power that allows us to pray and heal for those who are suffering.

It is a journey of development of character and the heart. It can be hard at times but in order to make us as like fine Gold, there must be a squeezing and pressure applied to our character that will produce a refined character in us that is upright and sturdy in Christ and not ruled by our emotions.

Servanthood, has a very high level authority attached to it spiritually because when you serve and are humble, the Bible says that the meek shall inherit the earth, you inherit a lot of authority in prayer and in your life.

Servanthood is not just serving it is a statement that says whatever position I am in currently and whatever my strengths are, I choose to humble myself and serve another.

This can be done on many levels from physically and practically to a spiritual servanthood where you might take up a position of intercession on behalf of someone else who may not yet know of the greatness of God, waking up early in the morning to pray for them. God's heart is touched by his.

God is a gentleman and he doesn't bombard our lives or our hearts, he waits for us to want him and give Him permission to move in our lives.

God sends us to do this person to person and build relationships, so that we are unified on the earth and as a community provide each other with family, love and support.

Because Mary's relationship with God was consistent, loyal and sincere, He selected her to bring forth Jesus. Mary became pregnant by Gods will. We can become pregnant (in expectation) by Gods will.

In Mary's time, there would have been great persecution for her, if she was discovered as an unmarried pregnant woman, but Mary asked God for clarification, trusted and relied on him and God brought a solution.

Pregnant women become hormonal and can be very anxious, when expecting a baby, worrying about baby's health and the life ahead. Mary remained composed and fulfilled the call on her life despite threats of breaking the law as she was not married even though she was divinely pregnant. God protected her.

The true test of our faith and trust comes in our obedience to God at times when it would be easier to do anything other than what God has commanded. I wonder what would happen if, like Mary, we willingly offered ourselves, without questions, to God's purpose and plan for our lives.

Jesus is our King and yet His desire is to serve us from heaven, how much more then should our desire to serve Him be. Hence, the fastest way to develop your gifts, is to serve!

Be Transformed by the Renewing Of Your Mind

Luke 1:38 *And Mary said, Behold the handmaid of the Lord; be it unto me according to thy word. And the angel departed from her.*

John 13:14-15 *I, your Lord and Teacher, have washed your feet. So you also should wash one another's feet. I have given you an example. You should do as I have done for you.*

Philippians 2:5-7 *Let this mind be in you, which was also in Christ Jesus:Who, being in the form of God, thought it not robbery to be equal with God: But made himself of no reputation, and took upon him the form of a servant, and was made in the likeness of men.*

CHAPTER 6 - SERVANTHOOD

Discussion Points

1. What is servanthood?

2. How was Jesus a great servant/leader?

3. Is servanthood easy, even if we are doing it for Christ?

4. How does authority increase through servanthood?

5. How is God a gentleman?

6. How does our obedience bless us and bless God?

7. Can anyone be a servant?

Activation

1. What has hindered your thinking about servanthood?

2. Recite a scripture that empowers you

3. Find a partner and pray encouragement and a blessing to each other over serving

4. Pray the affirming empowerment statement all week.

'This week I will serve others with love, even when its hard'

CHAPTER SEVEN

THE COMPANIONSHIP OF EVE

God designed us to be together on the earth. Eve is a helper to Adam, God designed her with a double portion of abilities that compliment Adam. Woman can multitask and take on Adams needs, and her own. Eve was called Adam before the fall of man, meaning that they were equally blessed by God. Adam needed a mate for himself, like himself.

We usually attract who and what we are!

It is not good for man or woman to be alone.

We need people in our lives to survive, to grow and develop. We need people who are the right match for us. Where we have unhealthy relationships, we begin a downward spiral that dries up our ability to love nurture and relate. Our countenance becomes cold and we literally become insular with nothing to give, no desire to share or love. Just caught up in our own emotions and reflecting on our own hurts.

The sense of touch heals. If you have ever seen an abandoned pet, it is hostile in approach because of fear the animal might even bite you in defense. The moment the pet is stroked and spoken to softly it is soothed and calms down allowing more love and care to edify it.

This is the same behavior for people. When people have had to endure life alone without Jesus, and unloved for a very long time, they build up a hard heart. When they have not been encouraged they are without compassion and live from a place of protection and withholding instead of self-assurance and giving.

It would take a smile or a single hug or act of consideration to reach the heart of those who are hurt and broken and relinquish warmth in a person. When we as a community fail to be a companion or friend to someone else, we have forgotten how powerful we can be in giving love, a love that is replenished by our heavenly father. Who has not given us a spirit of fear but of a sound mind.

It is challenging more than ever to have a lasting fruitful relationship on any level today because people have fear and memories of rejection and hurt that they have not gotten over and project these negative thoughts and fears on to others when in a relationship, which hinders trust and openness.

In any relationship if we want it to last, we must have a spirit of God's love, of humility, of understanding and patience and most of all prayer. God will move on your behalf to change the circumstances according to his desire for your life. Some will stay and some will go. In all the relationships we have, it is essential that we allow free will, we love and continually respect and we have understanding that not everyone is in the same place.

When you can be humble and peaceful about the character of those you meet, you will find that they are attracted to your light because you agenda was not to change them or have them conform to your ideals, but rather the stillness and peace you carry will attract them closer to a position where change can happen.

We want good companions in our lives, but God desires for us also to be good companions for others especially if we represent his heart but specially so that we can have the relationships we desire and that our lives are enriched by the flow of his love through us.

When we see something in someone that we don't like and point a finger, there are 3 fingers pointing back at us. When Gods reflection is upon us, we will reflect the nature of Christ through our countenance and lead by example.

It is wonderful to be surrounded by people who love us and have good motives towards us, in that place we can flourish and grow and have love to give out.

It is God who sustains us, even in a relationship. When we put Him first, he will direct our paths, give us a heart of understanding and make us a good friend.

Everything we have ever desired will come to us when God has been allowed to prune our hardened hearts, to realize our weakness and to engage in a time shifting from awareness of Gods power to thinking and acting like Him.

Not just to acquire his goodness in our lives, but to sustain His goodness in our lives. All change starts with our mind agreeing to change. God is always available to listen to us, and he answers!

Be Transformed by the Renewing Of Your Mind

2 Timothy 1:7 *For God has not given us a spirit of fear, but of power and of love and of a sound mind.*

Matthew 7:3 *And why beholdest thou the mote that is in thy brother's eye, but considerest not the beam that is in thine own eye?*

Proverbs 3:5-6 *Trust in the Lord with all your heart and lean not on your own understanding; in all your ways submit to him, and he will make your paths straight.*

Proverbs 18:24 *A man who has friends must himself be friendly, But there is a friend who sticks closer than a brother.*

We have fabulous minds, what we feed our minds results in how we think and what we think affects the decisions we make in the physical realm.

I challenge you to upgrade your thinking, to be conscious of what you believe and feed your spirit and act out, only that which is fruitful and Kingdom mandated.

When people are restored back to greatness. It makes strong communities, nations and Countries. When we are activated for greatness. Then we all will walk in the fullness that God has designed for us. Woman as the carriers, birthers and deliverers of the generations, you are what you think!

CHAPTER 7 - COMPANIONSHIP

Discussion Points

1. How has God designed us to find a mate?

2. How does our character affect our relationships?

3. How has God sustained you when you were disappointed by a friend?

4. How can you impact the community around you?

5. Are you good company to yourself and others?

6. How can you find companionship in Jesus?

Activation

1. What has hindered your thinking about your loyalty?

2. Recite a scripture that empowers you

3. Find a partner and pray encouragement to each other for loyalty and character building.

4. Pray the affirming empowerment statement all week;

'This week I will practice loyalty even when its hard'

AUTHOR'S PROFILE

Dr Yana Johnson Torregrosa, is an Author, Song writer, Keynote speaker, Entrepreneur, wife and mother.

She is a passionate Apostle, Business award winner and recipient of HRH Queen Elizabeth, England, MBE Honors award for services to Cosmetics. In her capacity as an influential marketplace Apostle, she travels with her husband raising up the five-fold ministers around the world.

AUTHOR'S CONTACT INFORMATION

To know more about Apostle Dr. Yana Johnson Torregrosa's publications, public appearances, book signings, book launches and many more, contact:

Apostle Dr. Yana Johnson Torregrosa MBE

Email:

info@dryanajohnson.com

Contact Numbers:

USA: + 1 347 359 4103

UK: + 44 (0) 7539 695 654

Website:

www.dryanajohnson.com

Social Media Contacts:

The Author is also accessible on Social media via Facebook, Instagram, YouTube, and other latest forms of social networks, as **Dr Yana Johnson MBE.** For direct communication with the author, you may invite her on Facebook and follow her inspirational posts.

Business products:

You may also purchase the books authored by **Dr Yana Johnson Torregrosa** either as hard cover books or e-books. E-books are available on Amazon KDP, Baines & Nobles, create space, Smashwords.com and other global e-book sites. You may also buy them directly from the author.

The Lord Jesus Christ is coming Soon!

END!

STUDY NOTES:

Made in the USA
Coppell, TX
25 January 2024

28198445R00087